Effective Speaking

Cristina Stuart is the Managing Director
a company which has enabled thousan
women to overcome their fear of speaki
includes several years as a journalist, as
radio producer of documentaries and current affairs programmes.
Since founding Speakeasy she has taught managers from many of
Britain's major companies and organizations as well as sales
personnel and politicians. She is the Charter President of the Carlton
International Training in Communication Club and a member of the
Association of Management, Education and Development.

Cristina Stuart

Effective Speaking

Pan Books
London, Sydney and Auckland

First published 1988 by Pan Books Ltd,
Cavaye Place, London sw10 9PG
9 8 7 6 5 4 3
© Cristina Stuart 1988
ISBN 0 330 29868 2
Photoset by Rowland Phototypesetting Ltd, Bury St Edmunds, Suffolk
Printed and bound in Great Britain by
Cox and Wyman Ltd, Reading, Berks

For
Mr Woo's mistress

Acknowledgements

The author and publishers wish to thank:

3M United Kingdom plc for permission to reprint from their booklet *How to make overhead projection transparencies*.

W. Foulsham & Co. Ltd for the quotes used at the beginning of each chapter, reproduced with permission from *Speaker's Digest: Business Quotations*.

Contents

Preface

The problem I have in writing this book is that you are *reading* it; I would much prefer that you were listening to me. I am a speaker and not a writer, so I'd like you to imagine that we are having a conversation.

First, I'd like to ask you a few questions. Do you ever feel self-conscious if you have to stand up and speak to a group, even when you know them quite well? Do you find it difficult to find the right words to express yourself clearly? Do you get unpleasant symptoms like a pounding heart, a dry mouth, sweaty palms or, worst of all, a blank mind? Are you sometimes worried that you might forget what you are going to say and make a fool of yourself?

If you have answered yes to a couple of these questions, let me ask you if you would like to have an inner confidence so that when you speak, you sound more convincing, calm and effective? Do you want to capture and hold an audience's attention? Do you want to think on your feet and speak spontaneously?

I believe I know what changes you, from an intelligent, articulate person under normal circumstances, into something else at the very moment when you want to appear at your best, and in this book I will show you how you can stop it happening.

Is this book for you?

Speaking in public

This book is not about public speaking, it's about speaking in public. It will provide you with basic techniques which you can apply in a variety of situations when you want to be listened to and when you need to be persuasive or convincing. For instance, you may hesitate about asking a question at meetings and while you are thinking about the words to use someone else asks 'your question'; you may give instructions that are misunderstood; you may already speak to large audiences but you want to appear more professional. Maybe your presentations to clients aren't winning as much new business as you would like; you may have recently been promoted to a position where you feel your colleagues are more articulate and fluent than you or your sales may be down and you fear you aren't getting through to your sales force.

Nobody is a 'born speaker'

We all admire speakers who can casually deliver a humorous, intelligent and well-reasoned talk apparently without effort. It's as effortless as a golf champion playing a winning shot, or an opera singer reaching the top note of an aria, or a comedian telling a successful joke.

It may appear effortless but, what we see is the culmination of months or even years of hard work and practice. Good speaking is not effortless, although to be effective, it should always appear so. It is a skill which can be learnt. You can learn to select essential points to persuade successfully, structure a talk so that your listeners will follow you easily and not be bored, hide nerves and uncertainty and show enthusiasm and sincerity. In addition, you can learn to develop an interesting speaking voice, make natural gestures and good eye contact, use visual aids and even cope with difficult questions. Nobody is born a good speaker. Remember what Emerson said: 'All the great speakers were bad speakers first'.

Everyone suffers from nerves

You may find it difficult to believe, but even the most accomplished performers on stage suffer from nerves. Laurence Olivier used to march up and down in the wings before an entrance in an effort to overcome his anxiety; Michael Crawford pants like a dog to release oxygen into his system; and Deborah Kerr calls it 'an unbelievable horror'. Their secret is in not letting it show, and it's a skill which you, too, can acquire. When a speaker fails to feel nervous, the chances are that he has become complacent and boring. You need nerves to give you sparkle but what you don't want are nerves which cripple you and prevent you from performing well. So in this book, I won't show you how to kill the butterflies but I will show how you can train them to fly in formation.

1 Listening: the first step to speaking

I do not object to people looking at their watches when I am speaking, but I strongly object when they start shaking them to make sure they are still going.
Lord Birkett

Is anyone listening?

To be an effective speaker you need to understand how people listen. If you don't, you could be broadcasting on the wrong frequency and you wouldn't realize it – your message may be clear and powerful, but is it being received? And if your audience is not listening, what's the point of speaking?

You can toss a cricket ball at a dart board and you may have a great throw and hit the bull's eye, but it won't stick. You may be speaking well, but is it sticking? Are you using the right words for your listeners? Are you structuring what you have to say so that they will understand easily? Are your illustrations relevant to them? Deciding whether to throw a cricket ball, a dart, a javelin or even a hammer is one of the skills of speaking. Choosing what you're going to throw depends on what you want to hit.

How do people listen?

Few people concentrate sufficiently when they are listening and so they become distracted. Principally by their own thoughts. This is sometimes called 'going down Route 350'. The human mind processes words at a rate of approximately 500 a minute but we speak at about 150 words a minute, so the difference between the two is 350. When listeners 'switch off' the chances are they are on Route 350. If you are sitting in a long, tedious meeting you may be thinking about a difficult problem which you have left on your desk and which needs an immediate solution, but at the same time you are listening, or should I say half listening, to what is being said by a speaker. You are going down Route 350.

Sometimes you're distracted because of something that the speaker says. He may suggest a course of action which you feel is unacceptable and you use your spare brain capacity to work out counter arguments. You've set off down Route 350.

Most listeners are not like dry sponges ready to absorb everything the speaker gives them. They are continually assessing, digesting, rejecting or accepting what they hear. They are measuring it against their own bank of experience and prejudice and evaluating its worth. Is this going to work? Is that logical? What happens if I agree? Is this credible? Not only are they judging the content of what the speaker is saying, they are also judging the speaker. Why is he saying this? What's his experience? Does he seem to know what's he's talking about?

So listeners sometimes fail to concentrate and can be distracted by their own thoughts, which may be unrelated to the speaker, or they may be distracted by what he is saying. They may also be distracted by his behaviour or appearance – why does he keep taking off his glasses – that's the twentieth 'er' I've counted in five minutes – brown shoes with a grey suit – what awful taste!

Listening is difficult

You may begin to wonder whether there is any point in your attempting to speak if no one is likely to listen to you, but bear with me because in the next section I'll describe the advantages of being a speaker.

For the moment, though, here are some other reasons why people fail to listen:

- They anticipate what is going to be said and switch off.
- They are planning what to say when it's their turn.

- They may be tired or worried i.e., they may have too much on their mind to concentrate.
- They can't hear or they find the speaker's voice dull and monotonous.
- The topic is too complex and difficult to follow.
- The topic is too simple and basic.
- The speaker lacks credibility and confidence.
- The chairs are hard; it's either too hot or too cold and the sound of the traffic is very distracting.

So why speak?

If you didn't speak in a business situation, how would you communicate? I suspect by writing; so what's the difference between speaking and writing?

The first major difference must be that speakers can see their listeners. As a writer I can't see you, but I'd like to know whether you are still reading this section or whether you have skipped forward to another chapter. Because speakers can see their listeners, they can react to them. I can't react to you if you disagree with what you've read; I can't give you any additional examples or different arguments to convince you of my point.

Although readers have the freedom to absorb the author's message at their own pace and are able to re-read complex passages, the author's words can't be changed to satisfy the readers' needs. A speaker has the flexibility to alter and vary his message for different listeners; complex ideas can be re-explained using alternative words and phrases; the advantages and disadvantages of a course of action can be repeated giving a variety of examples; the speaker can use the listeners' own experiences as support for his argument.

Your written memo might be misunderstood; your sales letter may go into the waste-paper basket; the recommendations in your report may be ignored, but if you present the same message in person, you are in a stronger position to ensure that it is understood, acknowledged and acted upon. Why should this be so?

Be visual

Inexperienced speakers generally rely too heavily on words, probably because they feel more confident when writing than when speaking, so that they overlook other factors which give a successful speaker impact.

It has been estimated by the Communications Researcher, Professor Albert Mehrabian, that words account for only 7 per cent of the speaker's effect on an audience. A massive 55 per cent of the speaker's impact comes from the visual, i.e. how he looks, facial expression, gestures, body language and posture, etc., while 38 per cent of his impact comes from voice; does he sound trustworthy, is his voice varied and interesting to listen to? This breakdown of the effect that a speaker has on a listener may sound unlikely to you. So imagine a situation in which you have returned a faulty item to a store. The shop assistant says 'I'm sorry. I'll see what we can do'. If this is said in an uninterested voice as the assistant leans on the counter about to resume a conversation with another assistant you won't feel confident that very much will happen. On the other hand, the same words expressed with concern by an assistant who is standing up straight and looking directly at you, will create an entirely different impression.

Here is another example. Think back to your favourite teacher or tutor at school or university. This first person who comes to mind is probably someone who was enthusiastic and animated; not a person who only relied on words, but who had vocal and visual impact.

If you are thinking that you usually don't notice very much about a speaker's voice, try recalling any phone calls you've made to people who are unknown to you. I am sure you made judgements and assessments based on their voices – she sounded friendly or angry or ineffectual – he was aggressive or honest or happy. Most of the time we are making these evaluations of people unconsciously.

In the same way listeners make evaluations of speakers. They might say 'he seemed ill at ease' or 'she looked very confident'. Often these opinions are formed before the speaker has said one word and are based entirely on the visual impact. Some speakers look inspiring and enthusiastic while others appear dull and insipid. Based on this visual impression listeners will have made up their minds as to whether it's worthwhile paying attention to them.

So remember that *how* you speak is often more important than what you say. A sound and well-reasoned talk can be ruined by bad presentation while a poorly constructed or unoriginal talk can seem entertaining and convincing if presented with vitality.

Don't be a writer, be a speaker

Throughout this book, I'm going to draw the distinction between speaking and writing because it's often wrongly assumed that the skills of writing can be applied to speaking. You should also be aware of the difference between listening and reading so that you can adjust your approach and successfully reach your audience.

Why is listening difficult?

- Internal and external distractions.
- Messages are received through filters of experience and prejudices.
- Listeners selectively listen to what they think is important or what interests them (two people in a meeting will often have different recollections of what took place. People working in an open plan office are able to not hear background noise).
- Poor speakers, i.e. dull voice, irritating mannerism, etc.
- Poor speeches, i.e. jumbled thinking, no structure, unsuitable vocabulary, inappropriate level for audience (too simple/complex).

What differences are there between writing and speaking and what different techniques are needed to speak effectively

- Writer can't see reader – speaker can see listener.
- Writer can't react – speaker can slow down/speed up/repeat and involve listeners.
- Writer relies on words alone – speaker can use body language and voice for emphasis and enthusiasm and emotion.
- Writer can carefully choose words but cannot change them – speaker can be more flexible and relevant by modifying and altering words and phrases to suit the listeners.
- Writer explains topic only once and reader can re-read – speaker must have a simple, easy-to-follow structure, frequent summaries and relevant examples because listeners can't re-listen.
- Writer has more attention from reader – speaker has to capture and hold listeners' attention by understanding their needs.

How to overcome the difficulties of poor listening by using the visual aspects of speaking

- Use facial expression, eye contact, gestures; avoid nervous mannerisms.
- Involve, react to and interact with the listener.
- Illustrate with visual aids, handouts and listeners' experiences.
- Use **enthusiasm**, **sincerity** and **vitality**.

Final thought

After a ten-minute talk listeners will have understood and re-tained approximately half of what was said and a couple of days later they'll only remember about a quarter.

2 Preparation and planning

Fail to prepare; prepare to fail
Anon

How to start

The deadline approaches and you finally sit down with a pad in front of you, determined to start preparing your talk, unable to find any more excuses for putting it off. You search for inspiration and desperately seek an opening line. If you're preparing for a large meeting, you may skim through a book of jokes because humour is supposed to 'warm up' the audience, but nothing seems appropriate. You may try three or four different opening paragraphs which all end up in the waste-paper bin. I'm not surprised, because you are starting in the wrong place.

1 Setting an objective

Before you start a journey, you need to know where you are heading and where you want to get to – in other words what is your destination? Later, you choose a path to reach this destination but if you don't know where you are going, it is difficult to decide how to get there.

Setting an objective for your talk is like choosing a destination. Before you even consider what you want to say, you must ask yourself *why am I speaking?* What do you want to achieve? How do you want your listeners to feel when you have finished? What is the reaction you most want from your audience? Allow yourself to day-dream on the ideal outcome of your talk. Don't worry about whether it's likely, or even possible, at this stage, simply identify what you want to accomplish.

Sometimes my clients find it difficult to pinpoint exactly what they want to achieve. They tell me 'I'm speaking because it's the Annual Sales Conference – I'm speaking because I've been told to – I'm speaking because I am the Chairman – I'm speaking because it's my turn', and so on. If you are unsure of how to identify your objectives, here are some pointers.

Start with general objectives

General objectives fall into the following categories:

- To inform/teach/train.
- To stimulate/motivate/inspire.
- To persuade/convince/sell.
- To explore/debate/negotiate.
- To amuse/entertain.

Writing down your objective in clear precise terms is often difficult, but if you refer to the general objectives, they may help you. Remember that you will sometimes need to combine several objectives. When I speak to the personnel director of a large company about my training courses, my objective is *to sell* training to him. However, I also *inform* him of the content of the courses, *inspire* him with stories of previous successes, *motivate* him by showing him how economical our training is in comparison with other companies, *persuade* him with logical arguments and even *shame* him by pointing out how poorly his staff perform compared with those in other companies. Remember that one general objective should predominate; don't confuse yourself with a mixture of too many general objectives, but always aim to include some entertainment.

When you write out your objective, remember it must be specific but also achievable. If your objective is to convince your boss you should have a company car (which may be an achievable objective) don't insist that it should be a Rolls-Royce (probably an unachievable objective).

Recently I was advising a hospital manager on a speech she was giving to a convention of doctors. She was concerned that she had nothing new to say and that she would bore her audience. She was unable to find the means to straighten out a jumble of thoughts until I asked her what changes in their behaviour she would like to inspire. Suddenly she saw how she could prepare a very passionate speech on doctors' attitudes towards nursing staff. Once she had an objective her thoughts became directed and fell into a logical sequence. When she had decided her destination, she was able to choose her route to it.

Another client, a managing director, annually 'addressed the troops' (his words). Each year he spoke for twenty minutes and although for many of his staff this was the only occasion when they saw him, most of them considered it to be a boring waste of time. I asked him how he would like his staff to feel after he had spoken. For some time he talked vaguely of motivation and productivity and feeling happy at work and finally he said he wanted them to understand how much he genuinely needed them. We then started to look at how he could achieve this. He had a destination so he could start examining the various paths that might lead there.

You may be saying to yourself that's all very well for anyone who needs to speak in public, but you only need to speak at internal meetings. I suggest that before your next meeting, you set aside a few minutes to think about objectives and answer the question, what do you want to accomplish by speaking? Is it to convince a colleague that your ideas are better than his? Do you want to stimulate a sales force? Maybe you want to impress your boss. Be honest and find your real objective. It should be:

- Written down.
- Specific.
- Achievable.

Where's the action?

As you set out your objective, be sure to identify exactly what you want to achieve and how you will measure whether or not you have been successful. Sometimes an action will follow. In selling, you know you have achieved your objective when the customer agrees to buy. But you also can have a fall-back position or a secondary objective; you may not make a sale, but your customer gives you the names of several companies who might be interested in your product. Your boss may not agree to a company car immediately, but does agree to your having one in six months.

You may find that identifying the action that you want from your listeners helps you to set an objective. Recently I was talking to a manager who had been asked to speak at a convention which was to be attended by politicians, members of the press and senior representatives of his industry. As he was uncertain as to what he should say, I asked what he would like them to do as a result of what he had said. He found lots of actions, so he started from the action and worked backwards. To identify the action, you must ask yourself how you want people to behave or what you want people to do after they have heard you speak. An office supervisor may identify the action that he requires as 'a decrease in the number of telephone calls which are put through to the wrong extension'. His objectives might eventually look like this:

- To instruct the switchboard operators on the new telephone equipment.
- To motivate them to take a pride in their job so that fewer phone calls are put through to the wrong extension.

When you have completed this first stage of your preparation, you should have a clear and concisely written objective which answers the question:

Why am I speaking and what do I want the outcome to be?

You might be tempted to skip this step as it can be time-consuming to write a succinctly worded objective which is achievable and honest. But the time and effort you spend on objective setting now will be saved later on in your preparation as it'll be easier to select material and identify key points.

2 Researching your audience

Now you've identified your destination, whom are you going to take with you on your journey? You are not ready to choose a path until you know more about your fellow travellers because paths which may be suitable for one group, may be inappropriate for another, so that you lose them before you reach your destination.

I can have no way of knowing if you are reading this book because you need to speak at departmental meetings with eight people or whether you anticipate addressing a conference of 80 or 800. So for the rest of this book, I'm going to use the word audience to describe anyone who is listening to you speak. You may feel that a bunch of your workmates doesn't constitute an audience, but if you are speaking to them at a business meeting, that is exactly what they are.

Whether your audience is large or small, if you're going to be an effective speaker, you must find out as much as possible about them. I wonder if you have ever had the experience of listening to a talk where nothing the speaker said was relevant to you? You found the material unoriginal and self evident and from the shuffling and inattentive audience, you judged they felt the same as you. Let me tell you that there was probably nothing wrong with the talk at all; it was simply given to the wrong audience.

I remember a group of bank managers who asked me to advise them on the presentations they were giving to school leavers. Naturally they hoped to encourage these young men and women to open bank accounts, but somehow they weren't having the success they had hoped for. It was hardly surprising. These middle-aged men didn't realize the need to understand their audience. It was no good talking about security, savings and pensions to a group of people who were longing to spend, spend, spend. Once the bank managers made their talk relevant to sixteen-year-olds, their presentations were successful.

Finding out about your audience will enable you to make your talk relevant to them and thereby overcome many of the difficulties that listeners face when trying to follow the spoken word.

Or, to put it another way, you should plan your journey according to your fellow travellers. Taking a group of school girls wearing open sandals over rough terrain is not impossible, provided you have anticipated that they will need to make the journey in short easy stages. With a group of experienced walkers wearing hiking boots, you could probably complete the journey in half the time.

What you need to know about your audience?

You know why you are speaking, but do *they*?
So ask yourself:

- Why are they there?
- What do they expect?
- What do they want or need?

Why are they there?

If you're speaking at a meeting in your own workplace it is possible your audience has no choice about attending – they are there because it's the Friday afternoon meeting; or because there is a threat of a walk-out on the factory floor; or it's the distribution department's monthly meeting.

Sometimes you have invited your audience to listen to you – you are making a sales presentation to a prospective customer. Alternatively, a client may have asked you to give a progress report on their project. At a public conference, your audience may have paid to attend.

Ask yourself whether your audience have chosen to listen to you and are there of their own free will, or whether they were sent – this can make a significant difference in their attitude towards you. Occasionally I find myself facing a classroom of antagonistic managers who feel resentful that they have been sent on yet another useless course when they have a desk full of problems to be solved. They are not receptive to my training and begrudge the time wasted on the course. When I am aware of this attitude I can try to overcome it.

What do they expect?

You must satisfy their expectations – if they are expecting a report on your experience with flexitime for office staff, telling them about the problems you have finding a suitable garage to service the company vans, will not be relevant. A group of business men expecting a light-hearted after-lunch speech, will not welcome a plea for more money to be spent on training for young people in industry.

In both cases the audience might well be interested in the alternative talk, but if it is not what they were expecting, they will not be receptive listeners.

When a client engages me to teach effective speaking, I know I can spend an amusing morning telling the audience of some of the disasters which I have faced in my speaking career. It would be entertaining but inappropriate if they were expecting to be taught; they might learn from my mistakes, but I would not be teaching them.

Beware of confusing your objective with your audience's expectations. They are not the same. A client of mine made a classroom presentation in which he identified his objective as: 'To convince the audience that Spain has more interesting holiday resorts than Greece'. He started his talk by saying 'I'm going to convince you that . . .' No audience wants to be told that. They want to make up their own minds. In the above example the audience wanted to be informed on the relative merits of Greek and Spanish holiday resorts. The speaker may know he is going to convince them but the audience resents being told so, and will erect a mental barrier against the speaker's arguments.

What are the wants/needs of the audience?

To achieve your objective, or reach your destination with all your fellow travellers, you must make the journey relevant to them. Your message must satisfy their needs. This doesn't mean that you change the content of your message, but simply that you put yourself in your audience's shoes and present it from their point of view.

I heard a manager arguing that he should have a car phone because all the other managers on his grade had one. He was refused. He didn't understand the listener's needs. He should have pointed out that currently he was wasting considerable time looking for telephone boxes which were often vandalized in order to keep in touch with his office, and that on occasions he had arrived at cancelled meetings because his secretary couldn't reach him. He could have said 'my wasted time is costing you a lot of money – with a car phone I would be more efficient.'

In general you can be fairly sure that one or more of the management needs listed below should be satisfied by your argument:

- Saving money.
- Increasing productivity and efficiency.
- Saving time.
- Improving quality.

If you are talking to your workforce, you may find that other needs are paramount:

- Earning more money.
- Recognition of work effort.
- Security of employment.
- Job satisfaction.
- Career advancement.

This is by no means a complete list; you'll be able to identify the needs of your audience more accurately than I can.

Recently I had to advise a client whose accountants were unable to convince applicants for grants of the importance of accurate form filling. Each form submitted had miscalculations, omissions and incorrect information which was causing more work for everyone concerned. Although the applicants had been told several times that the forms were important, they continued to fill them in with careless mistakes. We suggested that the accountants look at it from the applicants' points of view. What did they want? What were their needs? The answer was that the applicants wanted their grants as quickly as possible. The next question was how can this need be satisfied? By accurate form filling; and the accountants went on to explain how this could be achieved. When the applicants were shown how they could benefit from accepting the accountants' instructions, they were prepared to listen.

If you are facing an unwilling audience, you'll need to tell them at the beginning of your talk how they will benefit from listening to you. In order to do this, you must, of course, know their needs. With reluctant managers on my courses, I tell them that I can show them how to save time in their talk preparation; how they need never fear boring an audience; how I can teach them to overcome nervousness and how they can look and sound more professional. At the end of this little speech, I hope I have partially gained their attention and overcome their reluctance to be there.

What else should you know about the audience?

Here are some more questions you must ask as part of the audience research:

- How much do they already know about the topic?
- How much do they think they know?
- How much do they want to know?
- How much do they need to know so that you achieve your objective?

The last question is the most important but you can only answer it when you have some idea of the knowledge they have already. If you were explaining how new legislation could affect your company, you would choose a different starting point if you were addressing the personnel director than if you were talking to the warehouse manager. You may have been part of an audience or group at which the speaker assumed a common background knowledge which you didn't have and consequently you found it difficult to follow her arguments. Alternatively, if you are familiar with a subject, it can be irritating to listen to fulsome explanations. In both situations, if the speaker has not done sufficient audience research, he will be unable to make his message relevant and will lose his listeners, who go wandering down Route 350. The uninformed group will try to fathom out the speaker's meaning; the more knowledgeable one will be bored by the content. You may be thinking that with a large audience it is very difficult to find out all this information. But there will usually be a contact whom you can ask and at the end of this chapter I have provided a check-list for the occasions when you are talking to larger outside audiences.

In a situation when you know that there will be a varied level of knowledge, you can give enough background information to enable everyone to understand your talk without annoying the better informed by using the following phrases: 'As you probably know . . . I expect you're aware . . . Let me remind you . . .' For example, 'you'll probably remember that the dip in sales revenue last October was due to the cancellation of the large Australian order. I think we need to bear this in mind when looking at these figures'.

Avoid saying 'for the benefit of those who don't know . . .' or 'for the less experienced amongst you . . .' No one wants to be identified (even by himself) as one of the ignorant.

What is their attitude likely to be to you and your views?

In favour? Against? Indifferent? Openminded?

If, before you speak, you are aware of attitudes, you can attempt to overcome objections within your talk: 'You may be wondering how we can achieve this without taking on more staff . . .' 'If this sounds like an expensive proposal, may I suggest you look at it this way . . .' 'Many people say I look too young to have enough experience to cope with the problems of this department . . .'

Have they had any past experience which will influence them towards or against you?

Bad experiences colour people's judgements and often create an invisible barrier which prevents your message from being received and understood. You must acknowledge and remove this obstacle if you are to reach your destination with your listeners: 'I know that a similar experiment using temporary staff failed last year, but let me show you how my scheme is different.' 'Some of you may have given up using an outside contractor because of the communication problems that it posed. We can prevent this happening by . . .'

Here are some more questions which you should be asking

about your audience, particularly if you are addressing an audience outside your company:

- How many will be present?
- What is their position/occupation/title?
- What is their background/education/culture/race?
- What is their sex, male/female/male and female?
- What is their age?

Check list for outside appearances

On occasions you may be asked to speak as a panelist, as a guest speaker, as a workshop leader chairing a discussion or as an after-lunch or dinner speaker. Always ask your contact person specific questions and if he is unable to answer them, you should find someone who can. The more you can discover about the audience and the location, the more confident and effective you will be as a speaker:

Who? Find out about your audience; ask your contact person all the questions listed above.

Where? Exact address and telephone number, available parking, nearest railway station/airport. Type of room/hall/office/conference centre.

When? Day of the week, the date and the exact time.

What? The topic and any specific angle as well as the reason for inviting you.

How? Will there be a stage/lectern? Is there a microphone, if so what type? What equipment is available? How will the audience be sitting? In rows/semicircle/with tables?

Duration? How long should you speak and does this include question time? When will the questions be taken? Will there be a panel discussion?

Other speakers? Names and telephone numbers are useful.

3 A map of ideas

In your preparation you have chosen your destination and you've
discovered as much as you can about your fellow travellers. Your
third step is to study the map. What routes will be most effective
in helping you reach your destination? What material should you
include in your talk to help you achieve your objective?

You may need to speak in a variety of different situations, but
the method I'm going to describe for researching your material
can probably be applied equally well to all of them. From now on I
will refer to your 'talk', although you may be making a presentation, giving instructions, leading a training group, presenting a
report or making a speech.

When you have been asked to give a talk, the usual reaction is:
Why me? I don't have anything to say. When the initial panic has
died down, you'll probably realize that you have a great deal to
say and your real problem is deciding what to leave out.

Freeing the mind

I expect most of your original ideas come to you at inconvenient
moments like driving on the motorway in the fast lane, under the
shower or in the middle of the night. I'm going to show you a
method of capturing interesting ideas when it's most convenient
for you.

Unfortunately, much of our education has trained us to think in
a logical and linear manner. As you sit with a blank piece of paper
in front of you to prepare your talk, you may even start by writing
a (1) in the margin, but most ideas don't arrive in a numbered
sequence; it's difficult if not impossible to be creative and structured at the same time. So instead of forcing your creativity into a
linear structure, draw a circle in the centre of your paper and
write in it the subject of your talk and as you let your mind
free-wheel around it, jot down any ideas that come to you. Place
your ideas on lines radiating from the central topic. You'll find
that each idea triggers off others so that you can continuously
build on them. The advantage of this map of ideas is that you
have plenty of space to add new thoughts and you can also

'I suspect that most of your original ideas come to you at inconvenient moments, like under the shower.'

expand on those you have already jotted down. You'll have to avoid the temptation to reject material before you have written it down. This is not an evaluation exercise. It is simply a method of brain-storming with yourself so that you can put on paper everything that you know about your subject. You mustn't assess whether the material is relevant or logical – that can come later. I find that if I build the map of ideas over several days, new

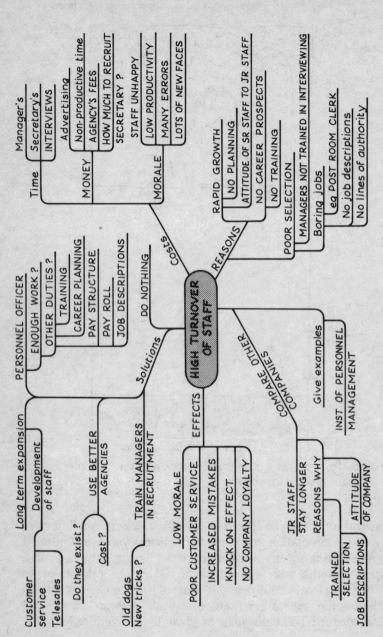

Ideas map

thoughts and angles occur to me at odd moments during that period.

Sometimes when I suggest an ideas map to clients, they dislike the concept, they find it messy or confused. At this stage that doesn't matter. It's more important that you follow through thoughts, views, opinions and information which may lead to examples and illustrations that in turn will help your listeners to understand your talk.

Too often we curb our creativity when we judge material as unsuitable or when we decide that it doesn't fit a predetermined structure. With an ideas map, there are no restrictions and every idea and thought has equal merit.

4 Selection

If you didn't like the untidiness of the ideas map, you'll appreciate the next stage in your preparation. Now you must look at the map and decide which paths or ideas are most suitable for your fellow travellers so that you can all reach your destination together.

Look at your objective and at your audience profile. Ask yourself what material you need to achieve your objective, knowing what you do about the audience.

You must assess each idea against your objective, always bearing in mind how your audience is likely to react. An idea which is totally convincing for a group of middle-aged business men may not be appropriate for a group of young male and female arts graduates.

On one occasion I heard a sales trainer advising a predominantly female audience that rugby and cricket clubs were useful places in which to extend their range of contacts. Good advice maybe, but not for that audience. So your first criterion must be to select material which is relevant to your audience, and which will make it easier for you to achieve your objective.

Secondly, refer back to your audience's needs. How can you satisfy them? Can you present your report in such a way as to show that your recommendations will save the company money?

Can you persuade your staff to accept the new schedules by offering them greater job satisfaction? Are you addressing a large audience consisting of people who want to achieve recognition in their own field? Any audience will want to know what's in it for them, so select the material which will satisfy their needs and their expectations.

Be very selective

If you overload your talk with too many good points, your audience will forget all of them. Remember that after a couple of days they will only have retained approximately a quarter of what you have said. You will be more effective if you choose one or two points, develop them, present supporting evidence, choose relevant illustrations, and recap and summarize frequently.

Summary of how to prepare

- Why are you speaking? Identify and write out your objective.
- Who is going to listen? Find out about the audience.
- Draw an Ideas Map. Don't be judgemental; be creative.
- Select ideas. Choose a few key points to achieve your objective.

In other words you choose a destination, get to know your fellow travellers, study the map and finally choose the paths that will take you there.

3 Building an impressive body

A speech is a solemn responsibility. The man who makes a bad thirty-minute speech to 200 people only wastes half an hour of his own time. But he wastes 100 hours of the audience's time – more than four days – which should be a hanging offence.
Jenkin Lloyd Jones

In this chapter I'm going to look at how you can choose a logical structure to help your listeners follow your talk, how you can develop key ideas and add supporting material, as well as illustrations and examples. This chapter will show you how to construct a persuasive and entertaining talk or presentation.

Selecting a structure

Listeners find it difficult to concentrate on the spoken word, so you must give them a framework. This is the equivalent of a contents page in a book or chapter headings and sub-headings of paragraphs. If you announce your structure early on in your talk, your listeners will be able to refer back to it if they wander down Route 350 from time to time. By summarizing after each of your points, you can lead them back on the main track with you. Remember they can't re-read your previous paragraph so you need to help them when their concentration fails. Your structure must be logical, simple to follow and relevant to your audience. Below I have listed some types of structure which you can use:

Problem/Solution This is a common structure often used in business presentations in which an examination of the problem is followed by a proposed solution. If you are suffering a high turnover of staff, you could describe the problem and show how to resolve it by proposing a more selective recruiting programme. If your company has a low profile in the trade press, you could outline the current situation and suggest a public relations campaign to improve its image. A variation on this structure can be used when you are in a competitive situation – describe the problem, examine a number of possible solutions, pointing out the weaknesses of each and finally present your own solution emphasizing all the advantages.

Chronological structure In this method the key points are given in a natural time-sequence order. For instance, you could state the origins of the problem and how it developed over the course of a number of years. This is useful if you want to set it in an historical context. It is also helpful when you are instructing or training as you can demonstrate the sequence of steps or stages in a particular process. Audiences find it easy to follow a logical time pattern. Presenting ideas and facts in a chronological order. However, it doesn't allow you to indicate their importance in relation to one another. Your second and fourth points may be more important than the points which precede them, but this won't be apparent from the order in which you present them. You can overcome this disadvantage in your final conclusion by emphasizing the areas which you feel are most significant.

Topical structure Also known as the qualitative structure, you list your points in their order of significance with the most important at the beginning. This is useful when you think your audience may not concentrate through your entire talk and are likely to pay more attention in the first few minutes. Generally, the listener's attention is keenest at the beginning of a talk and therefore it's prudent to take advantage of this. Remember that, in selecting your most telling or vital idea, you must refer back to your objective.

Spatial structure In this structure you can either begin with the particular and move to the general or alternatively examine the big picture first and then show how it applies to the audience. For example, you may want to analyse the sales pattern for the past six months and then put it into the context of the previous three years. You could present new taxation legislation in broad terms and then explain how it would apply in two particular situations.

Theory/Practice In this structure you outline the theory and then show how it works in practice. It's often beneficial to link the theory to what the audience already knows about the subject and then progress on to the less familiar. I saw a trainer instructing a young group of new employees in basic telephone manners. He asked them to recall situations when they had been treated well on the telephone and also occasions when they had had to wait unnecessarily. He checked what impression they had of the companies with which they had been dealing. From their personal experience he was able to demonstrate the importance of dealing efficiently with the public on the telephone. He went on to show them the techniques they should use in future on the telephone, in order to create a positive company image.

I have suggested that you choose a suitable structure at this stage in your preparation, because it enables you to place your ideas in the correct order. If you are undecided on your structure, try writing out your main points on several small cards so that you can change them about easily and experiment with a variety of different sequences.

Developing key ideas

The next preparation step will depend on the type of talk you are giving. If you are merely speaking for a few minutes at an internal meeting, you may find that you only need to note down a few selected points from your ideas map, choose the sequence which will be most logical for your audience, and your preparation will be complete.

Alternatively, if you are addressing a conference of several hundred people, or bidding for a vital contract you will want to plan in more detail how you can develop and support your main points and present them in the more positive way.

Think around your key ideas. If your colleagues have some

experience of the topic, talk to them, as an exchange of views can often stimulate a new train of thought; do write down any of the examples or illustrations which will help you to emphasize a particular point.

Occasionally when I am preparing a talk, I use a tape recorder at this stage. Imagine that one member of your audience is seated in front of you and you have the opportunity of speaking to him or her on a one-to-one basis. Switch on your tape recorder and talk around your key points. At first you will feel inhibited but persevere as you may find that talking aloud opens up previously untapped areas of material and releases ideas which you had stored at the back of your mind. Remember that the purpose of this exercise is to expand the key ideas which you have already selected; you should be researching ways of presenting these main points so that your audience is totally involved and persuaded by you. Try to avoid adding new main points at this juncture. A rough guide is one point per five minutes with a maximum of five points in thirty minutes. You should avoid speaking for more than twenty minutes, but if this isn't possible, consider using two or three speakers to add variety.

Each of your key ideas is a mini speech and needs to be introduced, developed and concluded; they should be linked together and should have two or three minor points to support them. If you want to write out your talk, some of the suggestions in the following chapter on Writing a Talk may help you. Alternatively, you can write out your main points on white cards (*see* confidence cards in the chapter on Delivery Methods and Systems).

Are there any grey patches?

Once you have written or outlined the body of your talk, try to identify where the dull patches occur; you are unlikely to maintain a high level of concentration from your listeners throughout your talk and therefore you need to add colour and sweeteners to stimulate their interest. The graph opposite demonstrates this.

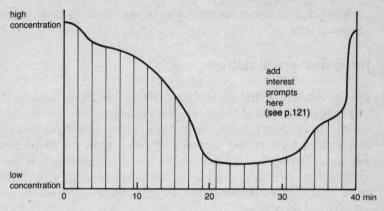

Concentration curve of audiences

Aim for a variety of facts, personal illustrations, examples and explanations. It's this mixture which holds an audience's attention. Some of your material may be heavy and difficult to digest so intersperse it with some lightweight examples to make it more acceptable to your audience. Try to break up chunks of essential but dry information with illustrations which are relevant to your listeners. Ask yourself whether some of your points could be better explained with the use of a visual aid. Remember that a visual aid should be a visual expression of an idea which you have used words to describe. It should not be a repetition of the words which you have spoken. Ask yourself whether your audience would find it easier to follow your talk if they had a handout or a chart or a table of figures to refer to?

Is there a natural break between two points where it would be worthwhile asking the audience some questions? Are there any other audience-involving techniques which you could use to break up the presentation? Even changing your physical position helps the audience to maintain their attention. Too much movement is distracting but an occasional change of position from one side of the room or platform to the other enables the audience to refocus.

You only need to consider these suggestions for varying the mixture within your talk if you are speaking for over five minutes.

Under this time the content should be sufficient to keep your listeners alert.

Jim Bains' presentation

The illustration of the ideas map on Page 20 shows how one manager brainstormed the problem of a constant turnover of staff which his company faced, on the ideas map Jim Bains jotted down all aspects of the problem, together with his ideas for solving it. He wanted to convince his board of directors that the company needed to employ a trained personnel officer but he knew that they considered this an unnecessary expense for a company of their size.

Jim decided that a problem/solution structure most suited his ten-minute presentation but he also wanted to use some of the other structures to develop his key points. He felt that as the overriding objection to employing a personnel officer was financial, he needed to show how much the continual recruitment of staff had cost the company in the past.

■ Jim's objective: To convince the board of directors that the company could save time and money and create a happier and more productive workforce by appointing a personnel officer.
■ How did he achieve this objective? By demonstrating the real cost of recruiting staff under the present system.
■ What action did he want which would indicate that he had achieved his objective? Agreement for him to place an advertisement for a personnel officer.

Below is the outline for his talk showing how he developed each of his key points:

1 The problem

(i) How it developed (chronological structure, past–present)

Small family run company with loyal staff; sudden rapid growth; inadequate job descriptions; poorly recruited new staff; insufficient training; dissatisfaction and low morale among employees.

(ii) Cost in time and money of recruiting (spatial structure)

Cost of advertisements; secretary's time handling responses to advertisement; manager's time interviewing candidates; non-productive time for training.

Use flip chart to show true costs of recruiting one secretary. In one year thirty junior staff replaced e.g. post-room clerk changed five times. Show total cost over a twelve-month period of recruiting thirty people.

(iii) Why don't staff stay longer? (topical structure)

Poor recruitment because managers not trained as interviewers; unclear lines of authority, e.g. warehouse packing clerk should help post room on busy days, but who decides? poor job descriptions e.g. relief work on switchboard done as a favour and causes resentment; no formal wages structure, e.g. pay increases apparently given at the whim of manager resulting in complaints of favouritism; staff with the company for three years accused of not welcoming newcomers; senior staff don't know names of junior staff.

2 Solution

(v) Personnel Officer (chronological present–future)

Show main advantages to solving the current problem; overcome any objections regarding costs i.e. refer to the high cost of recruiting new staff. Other advantages; some departments will be more productive as some aspects of their present work will be handled by personnel officer e.g. Accounts Department and the pay roll, secretaries will not be involved in recruiting; central pay structure – fewer complaints; proper job descriptions – less friction; recruiting with career development in mind e.g. Customer Service Department currently handles telephoned complaints, with sales training, they could develop telephone selling skills; long-term planning and expansion easier without present difficulties.

You can see from the above example how Jim selected some of the key ideas and developed them to achieve his objective.

He chose to use the flip chart to demonstrate the actual cost of recruiting one secretary as spoken numbers are difficult to comprehend and retain. If a flip chart hadn't been available, he could have prepared a handout showing a breakdown of his calculations to help his audience follow his arguments.

In order that his presentation should not become too theoretical, he gave several examples and illustrations to make it come alive for his listeners, e.g. post-room clerk etc.

Although all the ideas on his ideas map were valid and interesting, you will see that because he wanted to speak only for ten minutes he had to reject some of them, but he made sure that the file which he took to the meeting contained the additional information in case he was asked questions about it.

Later on in this chapter you will see how Jim chose to begin and conclude his presentation.

How to start

You may have forgotten that this was the title of the first section on Preparation and Planning. I hope you can see why you need to spend sufficient time and effort on the body of your talk before you reach the stage where you can choose the opening sentences of your talk.

What should your opening words say?

In some ways your opening words are your most important. Although people only half-listen to the content, it's at this stage that they are assessing how much of their mental energy you deserve. You will already have made a first impression before you actually say one word and as they hear your voice (maybe for the first time) you will be failing or passing the next test. How interesting are you? Are you worth listening to? Do you have **enthusiasm**, **sincerity** and **vitality**?

Your first few words must create a stillness as the audience prick up their ears and wait for your next sentence. You must grab their attention and suspend their questioning. Your opening words must be imaginative, stimulating and above all attention gaining. Don't confuse your opening words with your introduction to your subject. That comes later. If you feel that this sounds too theatrical for your business presentation, don't dismiss the concept completely; look at the examples below and consider whether you could use one or several of them to make your next talk more entertaining.

Your opening words to your audience must be enticing, seductive and should make them want to listen to you. You need to capture their attention, stop their minds wandering and show them you're worth listening to. A tall order, but essential if you expect to achieve your objectives.

It's as simple as A, B, C, and D:

*A*ttention – capture their attention
*B*enefits – show them what they will gain from listening
*C*redentials – give them your credentials for speaking
*D*irection and destination – tell them your structure

This may seem a lot to fit into one paragraph but it can be covered in less than a minute. I have described below these four ingredients in more detail, because from my own experience I know that your opening few sentences can be crucial to the success of your talk.

1 How to capture their attention

Ask a question

'Do you know how many phone calls the accounts department receives every day?'

'Can you remember what you were doing on Tuesday 11 August last year?'

'Have you any idea how many hours you spend in your car each week?'

As you read through those questions, you may have quickly thought of your own answers and that is what the audience does or else they listen for an answer from the speaker. Questions engage the minds of the audience and make them concentrate. *Don't* make your opening question too involved otherwise they will be working out the answer and won't be listening to your next sentence; *do* make the question relevant to the audience.

Quotation

'The brain is a wonderful organ – it begins working the moment you are born and goes on working perfectly until the moment that you have to stand up and speak in public.'

'There are two kinds of men who never amount to much; those who cannot do what they are told and those who can do nothing else.'

'Doing business without advertising is like winking in the dark – you know what you are doing but no one else does.'

Bookshops and libraries are full of books of quotations and you'll find you can spend hours looking for an appropriate opening for your talk. I usually hear pithy and amusing quotations from other speakers so I keep a file of anecdotes and quotes which I can refer to when I get stuck. Many of the modern dictionaries of quotations are compiled by subject which reduces your research time. Some quotes benefit from your giving their author and you can preface your remark with 'I like the advice that Mark Twain gave on Public Speaking – The right word may be effective, but no word can ever be as effective as a mighty, timed pause'.

Anecdotes

A short story which launches you quickly into the subject matter of your talk is useful, provided it is relevant to the audience and to your topic. Here is an extract from a story I heard at a meeting of personnel managers in which the speaker introduced his talk by describing the impossibly high expectations of some of the applicants for a recently advertised job. 'One young man said that he liked the sound of the job but that at his last employment he was paid more and the conditions were better, I asked him what they were and he told me that he was given free life insurance, and was enrolled in a private health scheme and that every year there was a 10 per cent bonus at Christmas, six weeks paid holiday a year, free travel and every Friday they finished at 3.00 p.m. I said to him, "It sounds perfect, why on earth did you leave?" He looked at me sheepishly and said "They went bust".'

On another occasion I heard a speaker open his talk on Business Acumen with this true story. 'Once upon a time there were two soft drinks companies. One got into deep financial trouble and the other was offered the opportunity to buy them out. The successful company figured the unsuccessful one couldn't last long and turned down the takeover opportunity. The successful company was Coca Cola and the other one was Pepsi. Somewhere someone must be kicking himself.'

If you are using second-hand material, try to personalize it so that it appears to be your own experience. But it is generally better to use your own stories, provided you cut out any irrelevant detail. In the Chapter on Humour, you'll see that the most successful anecdotes are those which you tell against yourself.

Shock openings

These can be fun, but you must be confident and deliver your words carefully so that their full impact is felt by the audience. For instance, 'You are wasting your time sitting here listening to me (pause) unless you're prepared to act on my suggestions'. Here is another, 'There is an epidemic in Britain that can't be cured by doctors but it's responsible for more lost man-hours in British industry than any other. Doctors can't cure it, but we managers can. I'm talking about backache.'

Historical background

This is a suitable beginning to set the context for a speech with a chronological structure. 'Twenty years ago this hall was a field and the idea for an industrial estate was being ferociously debated in the Town Hall.'

Current affairs

Sometimes a news item provides the right peg on which to hang your talk. Be careful not to use an item which has only just appeared in the news bulletins, as your listeners may not have heard it. You can find this opening useful if you are visiting a town and you refer to a local story; clients will feel that you are taking an interest in their area and not just passing through. However, do be careful to comment in a favourable way.

2 Give them the benefits

Once you have gained your listeners' attention, you must tell them why they should continue to listen to you. In other words show them what's in it for them. This only needs a few words but it reinforces the impression that you are worth their mental energy. Refer back to your audience research to find out what their needs and wants are, because when you describe the benefit it must be specific to them.

Here is an example of how a general manager began his talk when he was addressing a sales conference. 'We are going to double your commission and halve your targets this year. You may think that I have got that round the wrong way. I'm going to describe a new product which is so good that you'll only need to put in half the effort for twice the rewards'.

At a client presentation the manager of a mailing house company described to his client how he had reduced a competitor's mailing costs by half and promised that he could do the same for them.

In both these instances the audience may only half believe what they hear but nevertheless they are prepared to pay attention to the speaker. I had the experience of attending a conference for trainers where one of the speakers told us that she could show us how to save an hour a day if we followed her method of time management. I certainly want an extra hour in my day and so I could see the benefit in listening to what she had to say.

3 Show them your credentials

In your next sentence you should tell them why you are qualified to speak on that subject, what is your experience? A few words usually suffice to demonstrate that you are the right person. For instance, a systems analyst was addressing a School Board. 'During the last four years I have personally supervised the computerization of records in eight large schools in the region so I know the kind of problems that you are facing here.' At an insurance investigators conference a speaker explained his experience to the audience like this. 'While I was in the States I researched the methods being used there to detect fraud in insurance claims so that I am now in a position to compare their methods with ours.' You can use your opening sentences to establish a rapport with the audience and possibly overcome any prejudices which they may have towards you, as this speaker did. 'Like you, I have not been to university but I have done every job in this factory, so you can be sure I'm not going to suggest any changes that won't work.' By reaching out towards the audience, the speaker was helping them to accept his proposals.

4 Tell them where you're going

Tell them what you are going to say, say it and then tell them you've said it. The audience wants to know what's coming and it will make it easier for them to follow your talk if you share your map with them. It's not necessary to be very formal in this, as you will see from this extract from a warehouse manager's talk. 'I have two suggestions which I hope will show you how we can improve the layout of our stores department.' A distribution manager choose to preface her talk like this. 'The problem of incorrect deliveries has to be tackled in three ways:

- One, why do they occur?
- Two, what can we do to stop them?
- Three, how much will it cost?'

Jim's presentation

Here are the four opening sentences of Jim's presentation to the Board:
'Junior staff are costing this company five times as much as our competitors. Why? Because none of them are staying more than six months and some are leaving after only a few weeks.' (Attention getter)

'I'm going to suggest how we can reduce that cost and increase our efficiency.' (Benefits)

'During the last month I've talked to every department manager as well as many personnel managers outside the company, so I think I know what will work for us and what won't.' (Credentials)

'First I'd like to look at how this problem has developed, second how much it costs us, third why staff don't stay longer, and fourth what we can do about it.' (Direction)

End on a high note

Your listeners' attention will always be at its highest at the beginning and at the end of your talk, so you must take advantage of this and conclude with a positive restatement of your message. You will sometimes see an apparently confident speaker suddenly mutter a quick thank you and sit down abruptly. This gives the impression that the speaker can't wait to finish what was an unpleasant experience. There is no need to thank the audience and often these words are only used to help the speaker get off the stage and out of the limelight.

Your conclusion shouldn't come as a surprise. It should be predictable in order to allow the audience to pay maximum attention. It should be brief and not include any new material.

Below I have listed some of the methods by which you can end decisively:

Summarize

Use phrases like 'in conclusion', 'to sum up', or 'finally', to indicate that you are about to finish. Be sure to end shortly after these words – don't continue for another five minutes.

Ask for action

You can summarize and tell the audience what you expect them to do. 'I think you'll agree, having heard what I've said, that we must increase the budget for this project. Therefore I am asking you to vote for the increase.'

Ask a question

You may want to leave the audience with a question. This is particularly effective when you have posed a problem and have offered a solution. 'The question is not whether we can afford to increase our budget but whether we can afford *not* to. The decision is with you; what do you think?'

Use a quotation

Once again a good book of quotations will provide an ending which is humorous or profound, depending on the mood you want to create. 'Lord Mancroft once said that a speech is like a love affair. Any fool can start it, but to end it requires considerable skill.'

Tell an anecdote

A story told at the end of a talk must be short and emphasize the main theme of what you have been stressing. Remember to personalize it and make it relevant to your audience. After a recent talk on career development to a group of women managers I told them this story: 'Women are in a stronger position than ever before – even my young nephew has recognized this. He came home recently and told his father that he was second in class. First place was held by a girl. "Surely you're not going to be beaten by a mere girl," asked his father. "Well you see," said my nephew, "girls are not as mere as they used to be".'

Jim's presentation

Jim ended his presentation by summarizing his recommendation and asking for action.

'So in conclusion I recommend we stop spending unnecessary time and money taking on staff who are unsuitable and who leave after a short time. We need a trained personnel officer. I would like to have your permission to advertise for a personnel officer. In the long run this will cost us less and help to create a happier workforce which will lead to increased productivity and efficiency.'

Summary – how to build an impressive body

- Select a suitable structure.
- Expand your key ideas with minor points.
- Add colour to the grey patches using relevant personal facts, examples and illustrations.
- Choose a punchy beginning.
- End decisively.

4 Writing a talk

Speak properly and in as few words as you can, but always plainly; for the end of speech is not ostentation, but to be understood.
William Penn

Advantages of reading versus listening

Before I suggest some techniques on how to write a talk which will hold your audience's attention, I'd like to look at the main differences between reading and listening because you must put yourself in the listener's shoes if you are going to be able to write a convincing and natural script.

In an earlier chapter, I described the problems of keeping the attention of your listeners with the spoken word. Listening is not easy. Our own thoughts provide a plethora of distractions. Reading is different; if a reader is distracted, she re-reads a sentence or paragraph or even an entire chapter. I wonder if on the first day of a holiday you have had the experience of repeatedly re-reading the opening chapter of your book; you couldn't concentrate because your thoughts kept returning to the work which you had left behind and the possible problems which might have occurred during your absence. However, if your mind wandered, you could return to your book and attempt to concentrate again. Listeners can't do this. If they don't concentrate during your talk, they don't have an opportunity of re-listening. They only have one chance to understand what you are saying.

Readers can vary the speed of their reading and if the material is complex or unfamiliar, they can stop and refer to a dictionary or even discuss it with a colleague. Listeners can't vary the pace of the speaker's delivery.

Readers can skim-read in order to see the total idea and re-read what they feel is relevant. Listeners can't anticipate your total talk; only you know the complete picture and therefore what might seem clear to you, may be incomprehensible to your listeners.

So listeners can't:

- Re-listen – a reader can turn back pages to re-read.
- Halt or vary the pace – a reader can pause to discuss or digest what he has read.
- Listen forward – a reader can read ahead and skim-read, to select what he wants.

So, because listeners can't move backwards or forwards or vary the speed of their listening, what can you do to help them to follow, understand and retain what you are saying?

Tell them what to expect

If you give your listeners an outline of your talk or a map to show them where you intend leading them, they will find it easier to follow you. This is the equivalent of the reader who skim-reads to identify the main points before settling down to read the detail. Here is how one speaker identified the path along which she was taking her listeners. 'There are three main areas which the marketing department has examined over the past six months. Advertising, pricing and sales. During my talk, I am going to look at each of these in turn. Firstly advertising . . .

Tell them where you are

You can also help your listeners by summarizing and recapping so that they know how far along the path you have progressed. Here is an example from the same speech. 'So, to summarize our two main recommendations on advertising, we recommend a) more consumer advertising and b) limited but clearly defined trade advertising. So much for our recommendations for the first area that we looked at – advertising. (pause) Now I'd like to turn to the second area – pricing.' You'll notice from this example that the speaker has numbered each of her three points.

In her final summary, she looked back and told the listeners what they had heard – this is the equivalent of the reader re-reading to ensure he has understood. 'So the three areas the marketing department examined were advertising, pricing and sales and we are making the following recommendations. One, for advertising, we recommend more consumer advertising and limited but clearly defined advertisements for the trade. Two, on pricing, we recommend a new and simplified discount structure and three, on sales, we recommend a two-tier sales force.'

In the written form, these recaps and summaries appear repetitious and even unnecessary but remember they are not for the eye, they are for the ear. Listeners need these reinforcements to help them follow you as well as to help them retain what you are saying; without them, it is like trying to read a book which has no paragraphs or chapters.

Gather up your stragglers

You know that listeners are not concentrating consistently so you must gather them up as you progress along your path. Rhetorical questions are an excellent method of attracting back listeners from their mental undergrowth. You might ask 'so how do these new plans affect you in the sales department?' or 'why am I telling you about the changes in our budget forecasting?'

Listeners will concentrate on your answer because you have involved them with a rhetorical question and you have also indicated what is coming next. Use rhetorical questions throughout your script – they are powerful attention grabbers and signposts to what is to follow.

You can also anticipate how your audience may be reacting by saying: 'You may be asking yourself; so what on earth has this got to do with the Sales Department?' or: 'You may be wondering how much extra all these improvements are going to cost?'

With this technique, you are anticipating that your listeners are about to wander off your path into their mental undergrowth and you are enticing them back before they can stray too far.

Remember to recap constantly as you progress from one point to another; this will help people who have disappeared down Route 350 and may have lost the thread of your argument. Their own thoughts are continually interrupting their concentration and you need to help them follow the logic of your talk by signposting each point and recapping frequently. This speaker, who was presenting a problem/solution structure to her staff group, used a combination of recapping and rhetorical questions to help her audience follow her talk: 'I told you I would be tackling the problem of our lack of expansion from two angles: the shortage of available funds and overstocking of merchandise. First I've given you the details of our current financial situation. You may be wondering what these figures really mean? I can best answer that by referring to my second point – overstocking. Why have we a warehouse full of navy blue suits? Let me tell you . . .' In this example the speaker has reminded the audience that she will be tackling the problem from two angles; she tells them that she has already given details of the first point, raises their awareness of what she is talking about with a rhetorical question and announces the second point which she is going to discuss.

How else can you help the audience to listen?

Facts on their own tend to be dull and you will need to translate them into visual word pictures. 'Our warehouse handled twenty tons of merchandise this year. That's about equivalent to a row of eight-terraced houses' or 'our representatives travelled over 80,000 miles each this year; that's like going to Manchester from London 400 times.'

Try to illustrate with personal examples. This speaker was describing the drawbacks of being self-employed. 'Many people envy me because I work from home, but you know I never get away from my "office" and I find myself opening business letters even on a Saturday morning.'

Nothing helps an audience understand as well as personal

stories. I remember seeing a very successful sales rep graphically telling an audience about her first disastrous sales call and how she had gone home and nearly given up on the spot. It was her own story and all the audience shared her feelings of rejection and admired her determination to carry on.

The audience will always warm to you if you can reveal your own feelings and weaknesses. It can be difficult to do so. For this reason, the audience will respect your courage. Early on in my teaching career, I remember making a remark towards the end of a day's tuition to the effect that I had felt nervous at the start of the day. I was amazed at the number of people who were reassured by this comment and felt pleased that I was prepared to make it to them. On reflection I realized that it was because I had felt comfortable with the class that I was able to describe my feelings. If you build in a few self-revealing sentences, your audience will feel you are treating them as friends.

Use personal anecdotes to support your arguments. If you have experiences which illustrate your main point, the audience will understand and remember them more easily.

Use relevant illustrations

Make sure your anecdotes or examples are relevant to your audience. I heard a successful talk to a group of schoolboys by a management consultant, in which he compared management with that of being the captain of a cricket team, matching and balancing the strengths and personalities of the players. On another occasion a politician was discussing government revenue and expenditure in terms of billions of pounds; this could be difficult to comprehend for some people, until he equated it to the wages and bills which are familiar to every householder. 'Some bills have to be paid every week while others can be paid every month – but you have to make sure you save a bit every week to pay them.' The amounts may be larger but the principles are the same.

In a sales presentation, you may want to paint a word picture of how your client will feel if she buys your product, by describing a similar situation with another client. You could say: 'He told me he felt a great sense of relief after the new coffee machine was installed – no more rows about whose turn it was to make coffee'.

The majority of road accidents happen within five miles of the home. Just another boring statistic until a doctor friend of mine told me that if he hadn't been wearing his seat belt, he wouldn't be alive today. He had popped out to buy a newspaper and had had a bad accident. This was before safety belts were compulsory in the UK and his story removed my previous dislike of them.

I have heard a sales manager who appeared to be remote from the problems of his representatives, vividly describing the times when he was in direct selling and was required to achieve impossible targets set by his manager. His stories were relevant to the audience and illustrated many of the points in his talk.

Appealing to the listener

Put yourself in your listeners' shoes and ask yourself how can you help them to follow your talk and what will make it relevant to them.

Some speakers like to follow the FEB technique:

F – Feature or Fact
E – Effect of the F
B – Benefit to the listener

The method for using this technique is as follows: 'Because (feature), you will be able to (effect) which means that (benefit).'

Here is an example of this: '*Because* we have expanded the car park, *you will always be able to* park, *which means that* you will save time in the morning'.

These words 'because'; 'you will be able to', and 'which means that', are only intended as guides and you can choose your own phrases to fit the sense of your sentence, e.g. 'as the Board has accepted this proposal, you can start work immediately and say goodbye to your money problems'.

As you prepare your talk, imagine that you have to answer listeners who are asking 'So what? What does this mean? How does this affect me, my company, my department, my situation?' You should be able to answer those questions with FEB.

Talking numbers

In general, you should avoid speaking numbers. They are difficult to grasp by ear and can be confusing. Unless precision is essential, round up figures so that the listeners can identify them more easily, e.g. say 'nearly half' instead of '48.27 per cent' or 'just over three quarters' instead of '76.92 per cent'. Work out a method of showing a measurement so that it means more to the audience. From earth to the moon is 240,250 miles. That means that driving a family car for ten hours a day at fifty miles per hour, you would arrive there in 480 days, that is on 11th May next year.

If your talk must include figures, consider using a visual aid or handout so that your listeners can follow your reasoning more easily.

Size

This is difficult to visualize unless you compare it with a familiar object, i.e. smaller than a matchbox; about the size of two double-decker buses; as high as that ceiling or as long as this room.

Avoid jargon and abbreviations

Beware of speaking in terms which are unfamiliar to your audience – this can be very distracting and can cause many of your listeners to switch their energy to pondering on the meaning of a phrase or an abbreviation and so lose the thread of your argument.

Working with colleagues using terminology or abbreviations, which become part of your everyday vocabulary, you may be unaware that many people find them misleading or even incomprehensible. Carefully trim these distractions from your talk. Explain abbreviations at the beginning of your talk, if you feel the unabbreviated names are too long winded, but include the full name from time to time to remind listeners of it.

Convenient clichés or piquant prose

I've included this section because I believe that speakers can often be unaware that they habitually use imprecise words and hackneyed phrases which are boring to the listener.

Here is an example of what I mean:

'I'm absolutely delighted that so many of you could come here tonight as it's raining cats and dogs outside, but at least it's warm and snug in here. I've been asked to speak to you tonight and I don't mind telling you that I'm a bundle of nerves and I hope I haven't bitten off more than I can chew.

'I know I can depend on your support so I won't mince matters. Let's face it, things often get worse before they get better. So not to put a too fine a point on it, I'm going to ask you to stick it out. From the bottom of my heart, I appeal to you to put yourselves in my shoes at this point in time. Is this a fate worse than death? I can safely say I think it is, so without further ado, I'll leave you with this thought as I beat a hasty retreat, better safe than sorry.'

Of course no one would include so many clichés but it's often easier to use a familiar phrase than to find a more original expression. Try to avoid clichés which have ceased to have an impact – if you don't, your listeners will find you uninspiring and may eventually stop listening. It takes time to be creative and imaginative but if you invest in a dictionary of synonyms you'll find that your speech will become lively and entertaining and you won't need to worry about boring your audience.

Summary – How to write an easy-to-follow talk

- Announce the structure, i.e. where you're going and how you're going to get there.
- Summarize and recap frequently, i.e. how far you've travelled so far and where you've been.
- Identify each point clearly, i.e. landmarks of your journey.
- Use rhetorical questions to regain the audience's attention, i.e. signposts.

- Use examples and personal stories which are relevant to the audience, to illustrate your ideas, i.e. describe the beauty spots.
- Summarize the main points and ask for action, if necessary, before you conclude, i.e. recalling the landmarks.

5 Delivery methods and systems

Speeches are like babies – easy to conceive, hard to deliver
Pat O'Malley

Your talk has developed from ideas in your head to words on the page but until you have conveyed these thoughts to the audience you will not have achieved your objective. In this chapter I am going to describe four methods of delivery that you can use and I will explain what I consider to be the advantages and disadvantages of each of them.

1 Reading

This is the worst method that you can choose and you should avoid it. It is particularly ineffective for small groups but there are many disadvantages whatever the size of the audience.

An impressive speaker has **sincerity**, **enthusiasm** and **vitality** and unless you have a professional actor's experience like former US President Ronald Reagan you will find it impossible to express these emotions when you are reading.

Consider some of the other disadvantages:

- You can't keep good eye contact – one of the essential elements of effective speaking.
- Your body language is restricted – your script is like a ball and chain limiting your movements.
- You will sound unnatural and therefore insincere.
- Script dependence will mean you will never learn to be a convincing speaker or develop self confidence.

There may be some occasions when you can't avoid reading a

script and therefore I have included a chapter on writing spoken English (see page 178) and I have also listed some techniques to improve your reading skills (see page 282).

2 Memorizing

This is another method to be avoided because all your energy will be directed inwards instead of outwards to your audience. They will feel an invisible barrier and a lack of warmth, even if they don't understand the reason. Your talk will sound mechanical and will lack the vital ingredients of **enthusiasm** and **spontaneity**.

I remember seeing a speaker, who had a very eloquent and impressive style with well-balanced sentences and a wide vocabulary, suddenly start to stumble half-way through his speech. He referred to his notes but never regained his confidence. It transpired that he had a photographic memory and had attempted to memorize the entire speech but when his memory had let him down, he couldn't find his place in the script. In a second he lost credibility as he changed from being a fluent and articulate speaker to being hesitant and uncertain.

Although you may think you know your talk word for word, nerves can have an adverse effect on your memory and unless you are very quick thinking, you could find yourself floundering. By all means memorize certain passages which you are anxious to include but don't rely on your memory for the entire speech.

If you shouldn't read a speech and you shouldn't memorize it and you can't make up an entire talk off the top of your head, how can you put across your message?

3 Speaking extemporaneously (or planned improvisation)

This is the most effective delivery style as it has all the benefits of impromptu speaking and none of the drawbacks of reading. Your talk is prepared carefully with a punchy beginning, a logical structure and a conclusive ending; it's well rehearsed and you can use brief outline notes to give you the confidence to sound **enthusiastic**, behave with **vitality** and look at the audience with **sincerity**.

What happens if I forget my words?

All speakers who speak extemporaneously have a safety net and you must decide which type is most appropriate for you and your talk.

There are several possibilities. However, if you have dipped into this chapter without having read the previous ones on preparing a talk, you may want to look at them now, as you will find it easier to understand what follows.

How to use your ideas map as a safety net

You will recall that on the ideas map you put all possible facts and details about the subject of your talk and you didn't attempt to evaluate them or fit them into a structure. At the next stage you studied the map to choose the ideas most appropriate for helping you achieve your objective in regard to your particular audience.

If you are using the ideas map as your safety net you'll find the original map contained many fruitful ideas which were later discarded, so you will need to draw a second map which shows only the essential arguments and material. Draw the ideas in a logical sequence following a clockwise direction so that when you are delivering your talk you can simply glance occasionally at the map to reassure yourself that you are including all the salient points.

An ideas map has the advantage of being visual and displays your talk in its entirety. This is helpful if you need to cut or condense during the course of your presentation. The details of your talk should be well known to you, therefore you will only need a prompt of a few words if your memory fails you. Sometimes your mind may go blank between ideas; you finish one point and suddenly realize you can't remember what comes next. You only need a nudge or a few words to set you off again. Often it's the structure or the sequence of points which you forget, not the ideas themselves. The ideas map can put you back on track when this happens.

You may feel that an ideas map could be ambiguous or confusing – supposing you lost your place and couldn't remember which path you were on? If you are unsure of the benefit of the ideas map as a safety net consider some of these other prompts which you can use when speaking extemporaneously.

Your script as a safety net

In your preparation, you will have moved through the following stages:

- Setting an objective.
- Researching the audience.
- Drawing an ideas map.
- Choosing a path.

I have suggested in the chapter on Building an Impressive Body (Chapter 3) that you may not need to write out a full script, but simply note key ideas on to your confidence cards (see below); if you don't work with a script, you can't use it as a prompt. However if you do have a written script and you use it as a safety net this doesn't mean reading every word.

Use a coloured pen to underline the key ideas on your script so that they are conspicuous. As you rehearse, you should aim to describe each key idea and link it with the next one without reading or memorizing the words in your script. Simply glance at it from time to time to check the next point. If you employ alternative phrases and words during your practice, your talk will be fresh and different every time you rehearse. Using a script in this way increases your ability to speak fluently and decreases your dependence on the prepared text.

The key ideas are highlighted to assist you to follow your predetermined structure but you have the freedom to use your own choice of words to travel from one point to the next. Practise speaking round each point and don't be tempted to rely on the script; you should only use it as a guide to your destination and not as a vehicle to take you there.

Using confidence cards as a safety net

This is my own preferred prompt, as I find the ideas map can sometimes be misleading and the script safety net can be too detailed; confidence cards combine the advantages of both without the drawbacks of either.

You can prepare confidence cards directly from your ideas map, or from your full script. Remember that confidence cards should never contain full sentences as you don't read the cards – you only glance at them in moments of uncertainty. Eloquent phrases and clever ideas will only confuse you. Sometimes clients tell me that because of their nerves they can't see what is written on their cards – frequently I find that their cards are closely covered with fully written sentences. These are not a help – they are a hindrance.

How to write your confidence cards

Look at your written talk or ideas map and mark the key points in red; next check the links you have used to move from one point to another and mark these in blue. If you have included anecdotes and illustrations mark these in green. This will provide the skeleton of your talk.

Using 4" × 6" index cards write out in capital letters your key points, your links and your illustrations in the order in which they appear on your talk. Write on one side of the cards only.

If you are working from a full script, you must be very self-disciplined to avoid including all your persuasive phrases and scintillating sentences. **Only single key words will help you.**

Remember it's *your* speech with *your* ideas so you don't have to absorb and learn a host of alien concepts which you might forget. You only need learn the sequence of ideas and the links between them to give a good talk.

I restrain myself from over writing on my cards by considering whether I would be able to continue my talk without a particular word or phrase. Often I find that I reject it because it's not central to my talk. I have included it because it was a particularly clever turn of phrase.

The test for the effectiveness of your confidence cards is how few words you have on them, not how many.

Why cards?

I suggest you use 4" × 6" cards, because they are less distracting than paper. You can hold them in your hand, or rest them on the lectern or table and you will look professional. Should you suffer from trembling hands, cards won't reveal this as much as a flapping piece of paper.

What's on them?

As well as reducing your talk to key words and ideas, on your confidence cards you can add instructions to yourself such as 'smile', 'look at the audience', 'stand still' etc., and you can mark the point where you want to use a visual aid or write on the flip chart.

Only two full sentences

Although it's essential to mark only key words on your cards, there are two exceptions to this rule. To give a strong framework you can write out in full the opening and closing sentences of your talk. You will probably find that your anxiety is at its highest point immediately before you speak and it's reassuring to see in front of you the exact words with which you'll begin. Similarly you will need a clear end to your talk and if the final sentence is written out in full, you will be able to resist the temptation to run past the finishing post.

Memorizing the opening and closing sentences can also be a boost to your confidence and will enable you to make positive eye contact with your listeners at the two periods in your talk when you know you are likely to have their maximum attention.

```
┌────────────────────────────────────────────┐
│  Remember                              3     │
│                                              │
│   II COST/TIME RECRUITMENT                   │
│      - ADVERTISEMENTS                        │
│      - SEC. & MANAGER'S TIME                 │
│      - NON-PRODUCTIVE TIME                   │
│                                              │
│   ┌──────────┐                               │
│   │FLIP CHART│                               │
│   └──────────┘                               │
│      RECRUIT I SEC. = £560                   │
│          30 × 560 = £16,800                  │
│      eg Post room clerk 5 in 12 mths         │
└────────────────────────────────────────────┘
```

Jim Bain's confidence card

You should also write out in full any quotations which you intend to include as it's essential to use the exact words.

Remember to number them

Although some speakers tie a treasury tag through a punched hole to keep the cards together, I prefer to keep them untied as this allows me to take out cards or add to them. If they are untied, be sure to number them, because dropping unnumbered cards moments before you speak would be a calamity.

What are the advantages?

Using confidence cards will help you to:

- Sound natural – because you will be choosing your own words as you speak.
- Be confident – because you will have a safety net in the event of a blank mind.
- Look at the audience – because you won't need to read a script.
- Use expressive body language – because you will be free to move.

■ Show **sincerity**, **enthusiasm** and **vitality**.

If you have to give the same talk several times confidence cards will allow you to use a different vocabulary and even different illustrations for each audience. This will help you to remain fresh and spontaneous and prevent the material from becoming repetitious for you.

Suppose I leave something out?

Clients who have not had experience of using confidence cards tell me they are concerned that they may leave something out. Sometimes a participant on a course will resume his place, having given his presentation and as the other participants are congratulating him he shakes his head saying 'no, no, it wasn't any good, I forgot to say . . .'

My response is 'So what?' If you omit a passage, no one is aware of it but you. It will probably be a tiny percentage of the whole and although you would have liked to include it, rarely will such an omission affect the total impact of your talk. Don't dwell on what you have forgotten – instead, accept the praise for what you have remembered.

One word of warning – if you discover that you have omitted a passage while you are still speaking, beware of trying to back track in order to include it. You may confuse the audience. Should you feel that it is essential and cannot be omitted, don't apologize for leaving it out. Simply refer to it as an additional point which your listeners may want to consider, and remember to put it into context so that the audience can follow your structure. Often listeners know that their concentration is poor and even if you announce that you have four points to make and fail to include one of them, the audience will believe that the error is theirs and that they have misheard you.

If you have never used notes before and have always depended upon a full script, I urge you, during your practice sessions, to dispense with your script and try a few dry runs using only your cards. You will feel a great sense of freedom after your second or third attempt. If you are not prepared to risk dispensing with your script, try reducing some of it to key words and bullet points. This will enable you to look at the audience and talk spontaneously from time to time.

Pitfalls to avoid with confidence cards

Using confidence cards effectively will allow you to be an **enthusiastic** and **sincere** speaker but beware of these pitfalls:

- Don't shuffle or play with them during your talk.
- Don't keep staring at them to avoid looking at the audience.
- Don't use fillers e.g. eh, umm, you know, I mean, etc. as you choose your words – remember the power of the silent pause.

Visual aids as a safety net

Provided you plan to stand or sit close to the overhead projector, you can write prompts to yourself on the frames of the transparencies. A few key words should be sufficient to provide a structure which you can follow easily.

Your transparencies can also act as a prompt but beware of using unimaginative and wordy visual aids simply to provide cues for yourself during your talk. In a later chapter on Visual Aids, you will see that they should contain a minimum of words to be effective. Using words on the visual aid merely as a prompt is a misuse of it and an insult to the audience. During a talk, words are for speaking not for reading.

I sometimes use a visual during a training session on body language. I draw a stick man on the flip chart and as I emphasize the importance of eye contact, and using hand gestures, I indicate these parts on the drawing. This helps to reinforce my message and also acts as a visual prompt for me.

Using a combination of creative visuals and confidence cards provides you with an effective safety net which won't prevent you from looking at your audience and using appropriate gestures.

4 Impromptu speaking

Impromptu speeches aren't worth the paper they're written on.
Lord Goddard

Good impromptu speeches are prepared with as much care as any other and delivered so skilfully that they appear effortless.

A true impromptu speech arises with no preparation time, although you can sometimes anticipate the occasions when you may be asked for your views. If the situation might occur, plan how you would respond. Remember that every day of your life you are speaking without preparation so you know you have the ability to do so. Don't allow self-consciousness to hamper your self-expression. Some speakers collect short quotes or anecdotes which they can deliver on the spur of the moment and which are appropriate for semi-formal occasions.

If you are asked to speak unexpectedly in a business meeting you can use one of the following techniques:

- Build on the previous speaker's comments.
- Summarize what has been said previously.
- Restate the problem and add your own views.
- Agree with the other speakers and decline to comment further.
- Use mental prompts such as why? how? which? when? what? who? to build up your talk.

Summary – How to deliver your talk effectively

- Speak extemporaneously.
- Choose a suitable safety net.
- Practise several times aloud preferably with a tape recorder or on video.

6 Body language

I always think a great orator convinces us, not by force of reasoning,
but because he is visibly enjoying the beliefs which he wants us to
accept.
W. B. Yeats

So far I have emphasized the importance of planning and structuring a talk, but you will never make a successful speaker if you
only have a good speech; in fact you could even be an effective
speaker without a good speech. Some speakers can spend so long
searching for the exact word, the imaginative example, or the
eloquent turn of phrase that they fail to pay attention to those
vital qualities which will ensure their success in front of an
audience.

Audiences are not impressed with words. They are impressed
with:

- Enthusiasm
- Vitality
- Sincerity

How to make a good first impression

Even before you open your mouth, your audience will have made
several assumptions about you and, in the light of their own
experience and prejudices, you will have scored plus or minus
points. If you think this is unfair, consider your own internal
conversation as you sit in a railway station or an airport lounge –
aren't you assessing and criticizing everyone you see? We all do it
as individuals, to everyone we come in contact with, and audiences as a whole are no different; they are curious about the
speaker who will be part of their lives for the duration of the talk.

You never have a second opportunity to make a first impression, so whether you are entering a room for an interview, an informal meeting or an annual conference, your audiences will assess you the moment they can see you.

Smile!

Human beings have a very simple way of showing friendship, and yet judging by how little it is used, you would think it was very difficult and very expensive. Smiling at your audience says **I am happy to be here and I am glad you are here too**. Now I know that you are probably feeling the exact opposite, but that is the very reason why you should smile.

Why let everyone know you are feeling nervous? No one can see your pounding heart or churning stomach or your dry mouth,

'No one can see your pounding heart or churning stomach or your dry mouth, so why reveal on your face the turmoil which is going on inside your body.'

so why reveal on your face the turmoil that's going on inside your body? If you think that smiling is inappropriate for your position or your subject, reconsider your view because I am sure your audience would like to welcome a friendly rather than an unfriendly speaker. Even an undertaker smiles in sympathy. Remember you don't need an ear to ear grin, only an **I am happy to be here and glad you are here too** expression.

How to make an entrance

You have fixed your 'I am happy' expression on your face. You enter the interview room, lecture hall or meeting venue and you walk confidently to a chair or podium. You are making a first impression so let your body language say 'here is a worthwhile and interesting person'. In a small group, you will probably be shaking hands, always remembering to maintain eye contact and murmuring pleasantries about the weather, the cricket score or your/their journey, as you sit down. If you are speaking at a large conference centre, you will know what to expect because you will have rehearsed your entrance already. (See chapter on Visiting the Site.)

Once settled, you can look around and take a few quiet, deep breaths. Don't look at your cards or even touch them. No amount of silent rehearsing will help you make a better speech at this stage. Instead concentrate on what is happening about you and listen to the other speakers. For many people these final few moments before they speak are the worst but try not to let yourself be controlled by feelings of panic – you should be well rehearsed and looking forward to giving a good performance.

Why is body language important?

However you look or move, you will be giving off signs to your audience as to your inner feelings. Being aware of your particular mannerisms and nervous gestures enables you to correct them and present a confident unselfconscious image.

In spite of my experience, I am always apprehensive standing in front of an audience, but people tell me that I look totally in control and relaxed. In fact I am in control, but I am *not* relaxed; that might sound uncomfortable to you as maybe you are aiming to be a casual, informal and unpretentious speaker. Let me remind you of the line attributed to Mark Twain. 'It takes three weeks to write and perfect a good impromptu remark.' I believe that nobody is born a good speaker and that you have to work at your body language to *appear* relaxed and natural in the same way as Mark Twain worked on what appeared to be a throw away line.

The perils of bad body language

If your inner panic shows itself in your fidgety feet and fiddling fingers, your audience will feel uncomfortable because they want and expect you to be in control. In addition, they will not have confidence in you, your ideas or your product or service. They will not believe in you, they won't listen well and will quickly forget what you have said. If you look confident and believe in yourself, you will have credibility and your listeners will be eager to hear what you have to say.

As you stand facing your audience, I don't think for one moment that you will feel cool, calm and confident – I expect you will be suffering anything from mild apprehension to abject terror, depending on the extent of your experience. At this stage don't worry about your *feelings* – the next chapter covers How to Cope with Nerves – for at this point you want simply to *look* cool, calm and confident. The rest of this chapter shows you how you can achieve this.

Eye communication

I could see it in his eyes

When I am training managers in effective speaking, I have to be very careful not to overrun my time when we reach the session on eye contact, because I am convinced that it is one of the most important factors towards creating a good speaker – and I love talking about the subject.

Why is it important?

Looking at someone demonstrates that you are interested in them. Consider some of the common phrases about people in love – 'she only had eyes for him' – 'they couldn't take their eyes off each other'. If you see two people standing together and talking, you can judge how intimate they are by observing the extent of their eye communication.

People can also use their eyes to give messages of uninterest. There is nothing more frustrating than trying to talk to someone at a party who is looking constantly over your shoulder and around the room.

Eye contact also denotes authority. Powerful people give more eye contact than those who are less confident.

We say that he has a shifty look when someone avoids looking at us, but we also tell our children that staring is rude. Somewhere in between a shifty look and a stare is the correct eye contact, and it varies according to the degree of intimacy in our relationships. With eye contact, we can demonstrate our concern, love, dislike, boredom, disdain, even hatred – 'if looks could kill'. **We express our emotions through our eyes.**

Where is the audience?

I'm sure you have seen speakers who stare at the ceiling throughout their talk as if their script were written up there in large print. For a variation they glance at the floor or out of the window to an imaginary listener sitting outside.

Some speakers follow the ludicrous advice, sometimes given to novice public speakers, to find a friendly face in the audience and speak to it. After a few minutes of continuous scrutiny, the poor victim is asking himself, why me? The rest of the audience is feeling excluded from what appears to be an exclusive monologue; finding a friendly face is unfair both to the 'face' and to the rest of the listeners present. Avoid speaking only to the most powerful or influential person present for the same reason.

Speakers tend to look at their notes, at the back of the room, at the overhead projector screen or even at a blank flip chart – anywhere but at the audience.

Why is it difficult to look at the audience?

Before I answer that, let me ask you a question. Do you want your audience to know that you are feeling nervous? No, of course not and that is the reason why you find it difficult to look at them. You know instinctively that you express your emotions through your eyes and so if you don't look at them, they won't be able to see how nervous you are.

Having people looking at you is unnerving, you feel put on the spot, cornered and trapped, so you distance yourself from the situation by looking out of the window. You feel, quite illogically, that if you don't look at them, they will be able to see less of you.

What happens when we don't make eye contact

People who are interested in each other, make eye contact when they are talking because they want to know how their listener is receiving their message. When you don't look at the audience, they feel (probably unconsciously) that you are not interested in them, or in their reaction to your talk; they feel the same way as you do if someone at a party talks while looking over your shoulder; they feel you don't care whether they listen or not; and because they do not feel involved by you their concentration lags. **If you don't pay attention to your audience, they will not pay attention to you.**

This was demonstrated to me recently, when a speaker deliberately only made eye contact with half of his audience during a forty-minute presentation. It was a medium-sized group of thirty people and afterwards when they were asked to assess the speaker, half of them found him interesting, challenging and entertaining and the other half found him uninspiring, boring and ineffective. You can guess what had made such a radical difference to their views.

How is your eye contact?

During the course of your everyday life, pay attention to the eye contact other people make with you and try and note how easy or difficult you find it to look at people when you are talking in a variety of different situations. Ask friends for feedback on your own eye contact. Practise maintaining contact for longer than usual without it becoming uncomfortable.

How to overcome your reluctance to look at the audience

Here are some games to help you gain confidence when you are speaking.

Look around the group and check what colour your listeners' eyes are; how many are wearing glasses; do they have thick or thin eyebrows; do the eyebrows meet in the middle? Imagine you are looking through a one-way mirror and they can't see you. These games work in a relatively small group.

In a larger group you can look at noses or at foreheads and no one will realize that you are not looking at their eyes.

As your confidence grows, try to look at their eyes and faces to see how they are reacting to your talk. In a larger group, you will need to make a W or M shape through the audience with your eyes in order to look at every part of the hall or conference centre.

I have spoken from platforms where the bright lights aimed at the speakers make it impossible to see beyond the first row or so, but I know that it is not apparent to the audience that they are invisible and so I look out into blackness and move my eyes around as if I am looking at each person present.

What to avoid in eye contact

Once you have conquered your fear of looking at your listeners, you must improve the quality of your contact. Little short jerky glances are not good eye contact. Remember you are communicating your interest in your audience. Sweeping your eyes over people's faces will not convince them that you are seeking their reaction to your talk. Practise looking at each person for at least two to three seconds. If this is too difficult at first, practise on inanimate objects at home or in the office. Learn to gauge for yourself how long a two-to-three-second eye rest is.

To check your eye contact after a talk, try to remember how each person looked – was the financial director frowning? Who smiled at your anecdotes? If you can recall their facial expression, you were making good eye contact.

Facial expression

Your eye contact is essential in audience communication, but if you are looking at them and frowning or appear depressed, they will not believe that you are enjoying speaking to them. So remember your 'I am happy' expression and if you have some difficulty raising a smile when you are suffering from nerves, look slowly at your audience one by one (this is particularly effective in a small group) and imagine that they are all sitting on the toilet!

When I was first promoting Speakeasy, (my company) I met a number of rather pompous senior business men who made me feel unsure of myself and, on a couple of sales visits, I felt that I had not presented myself well because I had felt intimidated by them. On the next occasion, I wrote a note on the top of my pad to help myself to speak to the man and not be overawed by his position. I wrote 'think of him playing football in the nude, think of him playing with a toy duck in the bath . . .'

If you find yourself in a difficult situation where you fear your own feelings may hinder your performance, play a game to overcome your doubts. Think happy and avoid frowning at your listeners – it's not their fault that you feel nervous. You may have to exaggerate your smile if you are one of those people like Queen Elizabeth or the Princess Royal, who can look rather sombre because, in repose, the corners of their mouths turn downwards.

Hands

When a speaker is fairly accomplished, it is often her hands which will reveal that she is feeling apprehensive.

What not to do with your hands

Fiddling with   rings, watch, cuff-links, buttons, pens, elastic bands, paper clips, spectacles, cuticles and nails, confidence cards, coins in pocket, pointers.

Touching and patting face, hair, pockets, desk, table.

Clutching back of chair, notes, side of lectern.

Scratching any part of the body.

Hiding them behind back, in pockets, in lap, by folding arms, or by sitting on hands.

Pointing at the audience.

Wringing in despair.

Rubbing together in enthusiasm.

'I am amazed at the range of activities that speakers find for their hands.'

I am amazed at the range of activities that speakers find for their hands and I am sure that you have seen living examples of most of those that I have listed above.

What to do with your hands

Keep them empty and still.

Your hands do not have a separate identity – they are part of your arms and, in general, only need to move if you are making a gesture, and should only hold your confidence cards.

Arm gestures

You will see speakers making small gestures as if their arms were paralysed to the wrist or to the elbow. It is all part of the self-consciousness of being in front of an audience. Somehow they feel that if they make small gestures, they will not be quite so visible to the audience.

Remember your arm begins at your shoulder – always use all of your arm. Don't tuck in your elbows to your waist or make jerky, half-hearted, meaningless gestures. I remember a tall woman on one of my courses who, through shyness, stood hunched up, making tiny movements with her hands. We advised her to stand tall, make eye contact and use her arms to express her enthusiasm. The result was startling – she became regal and was very impressive. Without even opening her mouth, she looked like a self-confident interesting speaker.

When should you make gestures?

When we are not under stress, our gestures coincide with what we are saying. We use them to emphasize a point: 'I won't stand for this a moment longer'; we indicate a place: 'the management out there think that the union members . . .' We can express an idea; a spiral staircase, or a size, 'we have an enormous majority . . .' 'The spare part we needed was expensive but very small'.

Some people naturally use more gestures than others; people from the Latin countries tend to use more gestures than those from Northern Europe. These are natural gestures and you should continue to use them if this is your style. Under stress many people wave their arms in meaningless repetitive movements as if they were trying to shake off a persistent insect. Watch yourself on video if possible, or in front of a full length mirror to check if you have any mannerisms you want to eliminate.

Useless gestures, as opposed to those with a purpose, reveal nervousness and become a distraction to the audience. Don't be afraid to use your arms, though, because standing rigid like a wooden soldier is as unnatural as waving your arms about unnecessarily.

What to do with your hands when you are not using your arms

Keep your hands empty and still by the sides of your body. This will feel odd, but it looks very natural. But don't keep your arms glued to your sides because, when a gesture is required, your hands will only make little waving movements somewhere down by your thighs.

Some speakers feel more comfortable with their hands held lightly in front of them at waist level – if you use this position, remember not to clench your hands together so they can't escape. If you do, your gestures will eventually show themselves through jerky elbow and shoulder movements.

Other speakers like to stand with their hands lightly clasped in what is known in the fig leaf position, slightly below your waist. Once again, be sure that your hands are free to make gestures to suit the content of your talk.

If you are holding confidence cards, be sure to gesture with the other hand, however you can change hands so that you are able to use both during your talk.

Position and posture

Avoiding barriers

Facing an audience, whether it is of five, fifty or five hundred, is difficult and speakers like to hide behind desks, tables or lecterns.

If you want to be a good speaker, you must learn to stand totally exposed in front of your audience. Always stand in front of all the barriers.

Pitfalls of lecterns

I am 5'2" and some lecterns are 4'0" high, so how can I be a powerful speaker if my listeners can only see my head peeping over the edge? Even if you are over six feet tall, try to stand to one side of the lectern so that you can refer to your notes and your listeners can see all of your body. This will also make it easier for you to make natural gestures and to move around. If the lectern is fixed with a microphone, you have no choice but to stand behind it. Stand on a box if you are short so that your upper body can be seen. Ask for a radio microphone if you want to move away from the lectern.

Standing and sitting

In the chapter on Audiences, I have referred to small meetings (about fifteen to twenty people) where it is customary to sit. If you can break this custom, do so, because standing gives you authority, enables you to breathe properly and project your voice and to make better eye contact. The disadvantages of sitting are:

- Your chest is restricted and it is difficult to use your lungs effectively.
- Your eye contact may be limited and you may be tempted to look down at your notes too much.
- Your listeners may not be able to see you.
- It will be very tempting to play with pens and paper clips on the table.

The advantages of standing are:

- You will feel more visible and have more authority.
- Your voice projection will be better.
- You will have room to make gestures (don't lean on the table or clutch the back of the chair if you are standing behind it).

Stand tall

Act confidently, even if you are quivering inside. If you could see yourself on video, you would be surprised at how little your nerves show. Push back your shoulders and open up your chest as if you are about to begin the first day of your holiday. Remember, if you look as if you believe in yourself, your listeners will accept and retain what you say. They are on your side, so don't disappoint them.

Finding your feet

Like hands, these creatures on the ends of our legs seem to be stimulated by nerves to act very strangely. I have seen normal men and women:

- Hopping from one foot to another.
- Taking two steps forward and two steps back.
- Standing on one leg.
- Crossing their legs in the 'I want to go to the toilet' stand.
- Rocking to and fro.
- Swaying from side to side.
- Flexing at the knees.
- Rising up on their toes on every third word.
- Rising up on their toes on every third word on a squeaky floorboard.
- Sticking out one foot and 'boring for oil' with the heel.
- Going on little undirected walk-abouts.
- Tracking the pattern of the carpet with the curve of their shoe.
- Walking up and down like a caged animal.
- Standing on the sides of their shoes.

If you can identify any of these traits in your own performance, I suggest you imagine that you are standing in weighted boots, so that it is impossible to move without a conscious decision. You should be aiming for steady, relevant movements not cat-on-a-hot-tin-roof jerks. You don't have to stay nailed to one spot, but you should be consciously deciding when to move to another spot – to the flip chart, towards a questioner in the audience, to pick up a visual aid – and you should not be at the mercy of your fidgeting feet.

Sometimes I find speakers who have learned to control their feet, but compensate by swinging their hips or swaying or even leaning to one side. Stand upright on two feet a few inches apart, so that your hips are balanced over them and your shoulders and the rest of your body are balanced over your hips. Don't slump or lean on one foot with your hip sticking out. Think of a core of calm confidence which is beaming out from the centre of your chest. Remember the following rules of body language and you are now in a position to open your mouth and begin to speak.

Summary – how to look like an effective speaker

- Use your eyes to make contact with your audience and show them that you are interested in them.
- Your face should say, **I am happy to be here and I'm glad you're here too**.
- Your hands should be empty and still.
- Gestures should start from the shoulder and be relevant.
- Don't hide behind barriers.
- Stand tall, don't sit.
- Balance on both feet and wear imaginary lead-weighted boots.
- Let the beam of calm confidence shine out from your chest.

7 Learning to cope with nerves

I don't aim to kill the butterflies, but I want to get them to fly in formation.
Anon

First catch your butterflies

In this chapter I want to look at what makes you nervous, how it feels and how you can overcome it.

Immediately I see that I have set myself an impossible task. How can I know what makes *you* nervous and how it feels for *you*? So you're going to have to help me and you will need some paper and a pen to get the most out of this chapter. Pause for a moment in your reading and make a list of all physical and mental manifestations of nerves you have when you speak to a group of people. This is your list. If you have trouble remembering, think of the last time you were embarrassed – *where* did it affect you? In your face? Your stomach? Your hands?

You might find that just thinking about feeling nervous produces some of the symptoms. If so, observe them and try to measure your level of anxiety on a scale of one to ten. One is the lowest level of anxiety and ten is the highest level. Speaking in public is never a ten because if you were trapped in a locked car on a level crossing with a train bearing down on you facing instant death you would be feeling worse. Speaking in public might feel like death but you wouldn't die; it won't kill you. In a survey in America, 3000 people were asked to list their ten worst fears and speaking in public came out as number one ahead of death, financial ruin, spiders and snakes. You may sympathize with this view but do remember that death is permanent and speaking in public is not.

What colour is fear?

Do you think of a colour when you think of fear? No? So try and describe in words what your nervousness actually looks like, what colour it is, what shape it has, does it move? Take it out of your body and look at it. Keep it there for a moment while I tell you some of the symptoms that my clients have come up with over the years:

- Shaking knees, palpitating heart and churning stomach.
- Tight throat and unable to swallow, dry mouth or too much saliva.
- Wet palms, feeling very hot, blushing and feeling cold.
- Blank mind, unable to focus on audience or notes and feeling faint.
- Stuttering, shortness of breath, nervous laugh and trembling voice.

You probably recognize many of these and you might even suffer from some which aren't on the list. I find that I sweat a lot when I am nervous but fortunately only under my arms and not on my face so that it doesn't show. I also find that my heart beats extra fast and that my stomach churns.

The colour of my fear and nervousness is black and dark green and looms about me in a threatening cloud and I think it's laughing at me, but you know a strange thing happens when I actually have the courage to look at it. It seems to become smaller. Try to examine your nervousness without allowing it to threaten you. Just acknowledge its presence without any dread. Just think about the feeling and try to put it outside yourself. I know it's not easy but the more you try, the less frightening it will become.

What makes you nervous?

I can't answer that question for you, so again you will have to make a list for yourself of all the disasters which could happen to you. *List as many fears as you can*. Remember it's the fears which are making you nervous. Imagine you are in your next speaking situation and you are feeling terrified, or imagine you have been asked to speak, or even that you are in a meeting and want to speak but something is holding you back. What is it?

Is it fear of:

- Forgetting what you want to say.
- Not making sense.
- Being boring.
- People getting up and walking out.
- Your boss thinking that you are an idiot.
- Your subordinates thinking that you are an idiot.
- Your friends/colleagues thinking that you are an idiot . . .

You may see from your own list that some of your fears are not unique. In my classes it's quite reassuring to find that many fears are shared; even the person who appears to be most confident worries about looking foolish. Everyone has an insecure centre. The next time you see a good speaker, ask her how she felt beforehand and if she is prepared to be honest, I am sure you will find that she too suffers from nerves.

The great truth

Now we have discovered the great truth of public speaking – everyone suffers from nerves and everyone is frightened of looking foolish. Think about that for a minute because it's very reassuring. You are not any different from anyone else. You may be thinking that if other people felt as nervous as you, they could not speak as well as they do. You may be thinking that your nerves are worse than anyone else's. They are not. The nerves are the same, the difference is that you have not learnt to control your nerves – they are controlling you.

Negative thoughts or positive power?

Do you dislike feeling nervous? You may think it's absurd to ask such a question, but try to learn to welcome your anxiety because you need it to be a good speaker. It is the force which drives your motor and without it you will be dull and uninspiring; you need to harness its power to give you positive energy or it will dominate you and cause crippling panic.

What are you really afraid of?

Earlier I asked you to look at the shape and colour of your nerves which may have been difficult, but now I'm going to show you how to get to know and understand your nervousness so that you can take the first steps towards gaining control and turning negative nerves into positive power. But I can only do this if you are willing to co-operate in a painful exercise. If you are reading this in a bookshop, I suggest you go to the cash desk immediately, because you will need a quiet half hour by yourself if the next section is to have any lasting effect on you. Take the book home and only open it again when you know you can concentrate on it.

How to control your nerves

Imagine that you are at your next speaking function, you are about to begin speaking, you look around and you see people waiting for you to start. How does it feel? What is your level of anxiety? And as you stand there, what are your fears? *What is your worst fear?* Can you identify it? What is the most horrendous thing that could happen to you as you stand there? Think about it in detail because it's about to happen. Don't close your mind to it, just let it happen and feel the total horror and your inability to control the situation. It is getting worse and you can do nothing. Dwell for a few moments on the feelings that you are experiencing as you imagine your greatest fear.

After a time you do manage to get out of the more public arena and you find that you are shaking all over. Never, never again you say to yourself, never again will they get me to speak in front of an audience. You feel humiliated, mortified, ashamed. Examine the horror and dwell on it – remember this is only in your imagination so you can escape from it at any stage but it might be best if you stayed with it for a few moments more. Imagine how you would feel, what you would say, what you would do, how you would live through that full terrifying experience. Put down this book so you can concentrate on your worst fear. If you can force yourself to face up to your worst possible fear, you will be a long way to controlling your nerves.

Recently when I ran this exercise in one of my classes I had a manager who feared the audience walking out – he gave presentations to audiences of 150 people – and imagined that as he was speaking first one person and then another and then small groups began standing up and making for the exit. He was left with five or six people scattered about a large hall. He imagined the whole scene, how he eventually left the stage, and how he felt afterwards.

A young woman trainer confided to me that she was always fearful that the accountants whom she taught might challenge her right to be training. 'What real qualifications do you have?' As she was self-taught she felt particularly vulnerable. She imagined the training room and the senior partner who challenged her. She imagined her bumbling answer. She imagined the terrifying scene as the rest of the group lost confidence in her and how she felt during the lecture and afterwards.

Let's go back to your most terrifying moment and imagine that already twenty-four hours have passed; but you have not discussed your disaster with anyone because it's still too painful. You feel you can confide in a close friend maybe and you relive the whole situation. It still feels terrible but remember you lived through it – *you did not die*.

Now look forward a month and imagine you are telling a group of friends about the experience and you find that one or two of them have had similar experiences and are very sympathetic. You are beginning to see this experience as an event in the past. Try looking forward a year, and in a pub or at a party you meet someone who was at the scene of your humiliation; he comes over and speaks to you and reminds you that he was present. 'Glad I wasn't in your shoes, if only you could have seen the look on your face – it was a scream' and you find that now that a year has passed you can smile and chuckle at the memory.

You may have read quickly to the end of this section to see what the outcome was going to be. I would urge you to try this exercise and examine your worst fears and feelings. Some people have told me that their job is on the line if they don't perform well at a major presentation, others have told me that their reputation as an expert in their field might be jeopardized, a major contract worth milions of pounds might be lost if the speaker fails to be persuasive. Whatever your own personal fear is, remember that it can't kill you. You will live beyond it and you may even be able to smile at the situation in the future. Remember that for this exercise to work, you must not stop at the moment of the disaster but continue through to the following twenty-four hours, the following month and the following year.

How could you have coped better?

Now that you have faced your worst fear and lived through it, try looking back at how you could have prevented it or have coped better if it happened again. You will be tempted to ignore it, but if you can have the self-discipline to confront it, you will find that you can learn from the situation. You will gain confidence by aiming at a positive outcome.

Try reliving your worst fear again. It may be too difficult to do immediately, so read another chapter and come back to it. On your second attempt, you can imagine yourself coping success- fully with a difficult situation. Once again, imagine it in full detail; how you felt, what you said and how other people reacted. Don't allow yourself to imagine anything but a positive outcome. You may need to pause in order to choose your behaviour or find the right words; do so. This is your fantasy so you are in charge.

I hope that exercise has helped you to see that there is life after failure. You have faced your worst fear, coped with it and lived through it, so you can now concentrate on being a success. Now you are ready to turn nerves into a positive force.

Converting panic into positive power

In this section, I am going to suggest a number of techniques which you can use to harness your nervous energy.

1 Practice – your best defence against failure. Follow the suggestions in the section on rehearsing and practise aloud several times in front of a long mirror so that you can become familiar with every point of your talk. Remember to continue to the end of it on every practice session, because you don't want to have an over-rehearsed first half and a poor, stuttering second half. Find out as much as you can about the venue, seating arrangements, lighting and equipment, so that you feel comfortable with it.

2 Visualize your success – create a picture for yourself of the scene immediately after you've spoken. Imagine your clients looking pleased and stimulated by your presentation, or your sales force feeling motivated to work harder, or your Board of Directors nodding in agreement, or a large audience clapping enthusiastically. Whoever your audience is, think of them reacting in a very positive manner. Try to paint a vivid picture of the situation, including your own feelings of relief and pleasure. Don't allow any negative thoughts to intrude – this is your success. The more you concentrate on this, the greater your chance of it becoming true.

3 Pretend you are an actor playing the part of a successful and confident speaker.

4 Remember a good feeling – think back to a particular personal success, e.g. the day you were given a rise, when you were praised by the chairman, when you achieved the highest sales. Recall a day of personal achievement when you were proud of yourself and it felt good to be alive. This is your own personal source of high self-esteem and you can tap into it whenever you feel a moment of doubt. You have achieved in the past and you can achieve in the future.

Coping with physical symptoms

If you know you sweat, wear a light-weight outfit and carry a handkerchief to dab your face and your hands if necessary.

If you suffer from a dry mouth limit the amount of water you drink. Instead place your tongue across your teeth and gently bite it – your saliva will begin to run. Another trick is to put the tip of your tongue at the top of your mouth and say a silent LLL sound which will also help you to overcome a dry mouth.

Trembling hands will only be noticeable if you hold sheets of paper, so use cards.

If your throat tightens up and your voice becomes restricted before you face the audience, try yawning to relax it. Lift your lips away from your teeth like an animal snarling, open your mouth as wide as possible so that the muscles on your neck stick out and you hear a roaring in your ears. Now the yawn should start to take over and it will relax your whole face, neck and throat. You can't feel tense while yawning as it is a great relaxer, like laughing.

If you suffer from breathlessness, take deep breaths. Shallow breaths mean that you sound odd and you feel panicky. We take in breaths automatically, but we have to think about letting the air out so remember to breathe in deeply and exhale deeply.

I hope that some of these suggestions will work for you but bear in mind that you are not aiming to kill the butterflies – only to control them. You need their power to be an effective speaker; so use them, don't be frightened of them.

Summary – how to cope with nerves

- Everyone suffers from nerves.
- Don't let your nerves control you.
- Face up to your fears.
- Turn negative nerves into positive power.
- Practice kills panic.
- You *will* be successful.

8 Finding your voice

Why doesn't the fellow who says 'I'm no speech maker' let it go at that, instead of giving a demonstration.
Frank McKinney Hubbard

This is not a book about elocution and I am not a drama teacher so don't expect me to show you how to develop a deep melodious voice, throbbing with emotion, if you normally speak in a thin, squeaky little voice. No matter how you sound, you probably dislike your own voice if you have ever heard it on a tape recorder. This chapter describes techniques to help you create a more interesting voice and avoid the faults common among inexperienced speakers.

Another great truth

Few people like the sound of their own voice. This is because throughout your life you have heard your voice through the bone of your jaw, while everyone else (including the tape recorder) hears it straight from your mouth. Hearing yourself on tape for the first time is a shock, so try to be objective about it. However, if you feel your voice is a serious handicap, seek professional advice and if necessary join an elocution class. Unfortunately, I can't hear you speak so I can't judge, but of all my clients I only recommend a small percentage to seek further help.

Accent

The most common complaint people have about their voice is their accent. 'I sound so posh and stand-offish' – 'I sound so common' – 'I don't like the way I pronounce my Rs' – 'My Northern accent makes me sound unintelligent.'

Regard your accent as part of your personality and only consider changing it if you cannot be understood. There are many examples of successful men and women who have made a feature of their accent. Lord Denning, Nye Bevan, David Bellamy and Pam Ayres.

Volume, clarity, variety

To be an effective speaker you need:

- To be heard.
- To be understood.
- To have variety in your voice.

How to be heard

There are speakers whose soft voices make it difficult for their listeners to hear them, even in a small group. In addition there may be background noise – road works and traffic outside in the street, air conditioning or heating noise inside, as well as the general office hubbub in the adjoining rooms. After a while listeners give up straining to hear the quiet voice of the speaker and indulge in some internal conversations with themselves.

With larger audiences, you may have to speak over the sound of late-comers arriving, the rattle of china and cutlery as well as coughing and nose blowing.

The secret of voice projection is to use your breath to support your voice as you speak from the stomach. If you exert pressure on your throat muscles to speak louder, your voice will sound strained and you will end up with a sore throat.

In order to speak well you must breathe well

Most of us don't use our lungs well. In our everyday lives we take short shallow breaths and only fill the top half of our lungs. Under stress we breathe more rapidly but because we are not

'There may be background noise, roadworks, traffic outside in the street, air conditioning, as well as general office hubbub in adjoining rooms.'

using the full capacity of our lungs, we become breathless; when we are speaking, we can even run out of air before we reach the end of a sentence.

The deeper you breathe the more air you will have to sustain your voice and project it to all your listeners.

Try placing your hands on your ribs and feeling your lungs inflate. Now take a deep breath and count aloud on that one breath. You should reach 30+ but don't cheat. Full lungs will enable you to finish long sentences with no ums or ers, will kill some of your panic and take the strain off your larynx so that you will be able to project your voice like an opera singer.

Imagine that the air in your lungs is like water coming out of a garden hose; it can dribble out over the lawn or you can place your thumb over the end and direct it to the furthest corners of the garden. When you count out loud, control your air so that you can extend it for longer and longer. Each time you attempt this counting exercise, try to increase your breath control to reach a higher and higher number and to extend your voice to the far corners of the room and beyond.

Projecting through a wall

Imagine that your voice is a laser beam and it can penetrate the wall into the next room. You will need lots of air to extend it in a controlled jet, past your voice box and unrestricted by your throat muscles and out through your mouth. Practise reading from this book into a tape recorder in your normal voice and then again projecting into the next room. You should be able to hear the difference as you use more air to carry your voice further and further. There is no excuse for not being heard. If you suspect or have been told that you have a soft voice, keep using more air in your everyday conversation. At first it may feel unnatural and too loud, but persevere and you will find that people take more notice of you and interrupt you less. If you develop a strong voice, you will be perceived as someone who is worth listening to and you will have no trouble participating at meetings. Don't let your voice drop at the end of sentences, but maintain the same volume right to the final fullstop.

How to be understood

Many people speak with their teeth together, hardly moving their lips, and then wonder why they are not understood. I've said that you should be taking in air and there is no reason to keep it trapped behind your teeth. You don't have to save it. Let it out as you try this exercise. Say the alphabet out loud, opening your mouth wide as if you were talking through a half yawn and imagine your jaws cannot close and your lips cannot touch, except on the letters B, M, P and W. Repeat the exercise using twice as much air and projecting into the next room; hold your pen in your hand between your lips to make sure they don't touch.

Try saying these sentences smoothly all on one breath, without pauses or jerkiness:

- No man would listen to you talk unless he knew that it was his turn next.
- It is always the best policy to speak the truth, unless you are an exceptionally good liar.
- One of the tests of leadership is the ability to recognize a problem before it becomes an emergency.

Lost letters and swallowed sounds

Clarity and good diction don't mean changing your accent or personality, but do mean positively pronouncing every letter and sound in order to minimize the risk of being misunderstood.

How to add variety

You should aim to add variety to your voice because even if the words of your talk are stimulating, if your voice doesn't sound exciting you will not have credibility and you won't keep your listeners' attention.

Some speakers have a naturally varied voice with what I call 'colour', while others have consciously to modify it to sound more interesting. Nerves can often affect your voice and make it sound more monotone than normal. When assessing your own voice, don't rely only on a tape recorder, as it is difficult to listen objectively to how you sound. Ask colleagues for feedback on whether you need to improve the variety in your voice.

If you want to enliven your voice, you need to vary:

- Volume.
- Speed.
- Pitch.

You also need to consider inflexion and emphasis.

Volume

We have already looked at how you can learn to project your voice so that it can be heard and so that you sound more authoritative; now consider the power you have to vary the volume. Lower it if you have an important point you want to emphasize: 'Now, I am going to reveal to you the extent of petty thieving in this company'; and you can raise it when you call for action; 'We cannot allow this practice to continue'. Allow yourself to be dramatic and vary your volume to add spice to your voice.

You may feel that this is totally inappropriate behaviour for the small group meetings you attend. Don't dismiss these suggestions immediately but think of some of the men and women whom you consider to be interesting speakers – you'll find that without it being obvious, they are using a wide range of volume when they speak. I'm not asking you to sound like a great actor playing King Lear or Lady Macbeth but I am drawing your attention to the importance of *varying* your volume in order to avoid speaking in a dull, flat voice.

Speed

My clients often find that although they time their speeches when preparing for our classroom exercises, when they present them in the class, they finish too early. This is because nerves affect their delivery and they talk more quickly. Learn to slow down. Speak at half the speed you think is correct and you will be understood better. Your words will be clearer and you will feel more in control. You can add power to your talk by slowing down and using pauses to indicate a change of subject and for emphasis.

Pauses mean power

You should slow down between words and between ideas. Remember how difficult it is for the listener to follow the spoken word, so make it easier for them by pausing when you are moving from one point to another. Novice speakers find pausing one of the most difficult techniques to acquire, but it is a very effective means of holding your audience's attention.

Use the pause to add emphasis to your words: 'we are facing a very dangerous period in the history of the company (pause) very dangerous (pause, and look around with good eye-contact) but the solution is here in this room (pause) in your hands'.

Silent pauses

Pauses are powerful only if they are silent. Speakers who can't bear silence, fill it with the noise of their brain working as they search for the exact words. When their brain gets into gear, it omits the sound of er and um and mm – non-words which convey nothing and distract listeners. Learn to think silently. In your everyday conversation, you may find that you are using other non-words such as 'I mean', 'you know', 'actually' and 'you know what I mean' etc. so try to eliminate them completely as they are unnecessary and indicate a lack of concentration on your part. Sharpen up your conversation and eventually you will be sufficiently confident to pause when you are speaking in public.

Earlier in this book, I said that our brains process words at 500 words a minute and listeners can be easily distracted by their own thoughts because you are talking at only 150 words a minute. This difference between brain and speaking speeds works to your advantage when you are searching for a word. What you imagine to be a full half-minute's silence in your talk, is only a second or two and is totally unnoticed by your audience. Time and time again on our courses, clients see themselves on video and are amazed that 'that terrible silence when I lost myself completely' turns out to be a passing moment. Remember, a pause is a compliment to the audience. You are showing you want to express yourself well and are taking time to choose the right words. No one expects you to be as word perfect as an actor – on the contrary, that might seem insincere – but neither do they want to hear your brain crashing through its gears with ers and ums.

Varying your speed

As well as using pauses, you must learn to change the speed of your delivery to add variety. Giving introductory background information and setting the scene to your subject may contain information with which most of the audience is familiar, therefore your delivery can be faster than that which you would use when you reach the main thrust of your argument.

When I referred to volume, I mentioned the dramatic effect of lowering your voice and also of using the full range from loud to soft; this can be combined with speed to make a memorable impact. Use a slow delivery and a low, soft voice (still audible) to capture the audience's attention.

Adding highs and lows

Many speakers find that nerves cause their voice to go up a few notes and if you want to pitch yours lower you can practise the following exercise. Imagine you have a large Chinese gong and you are beating it, bong, bong, bong. Say out aloud the words 'Chinese gong, Chinese gong, gong, gong, bong, bong'. On each 'ong' sound, elongate the sound so that you can feel the vibrations in your throat. If you practise saying this for two minutes every morning and evening, your voice will be permanently lowered for as long as you keep up the exercise. You can test this out with a tape recorder. Speak into it before doing the exercises and again afterwards and you will hear that your voice has become lower.

However, you need highs as well as lows so that you avoid speaking in a monotone. Allow it to go up as you ask rhetorical questions, e.g. 'How can we show we care?'

Inflexion

Here is an opportunity to practise using the full range of your voice by saying the word 'really' to indicate the feelings expressed below:

'I have just lost my job'	'Really?' (horror)
'You need to get your hair cut.'	'Really.' (annoyance)

'Your work is exceptionally good.'	'Really.' (pleasure)
'We will be finishing on time.'	'Really.' (Disbelief)
'Truly I am looking forward to working for him.'	'Really.' (Sarcasm)

Even a simple word like 'Hallo' can indicate a variety of emotions by changing the inflexion.

'Hallo' – pleased to see friends.
'Hallo' – male welcoming a female friend.
'Hallo' – surprised and delighted.

Notice as you say each of these 'hallos' that the inflexion to show the feeling is always on the vowel sound. Therefore if you want to give colour to your voice you should e-lon-gate the vowels. Try saying the following sentence: 'I want to stay here for ever and ever' as 'I waaant to staaay heeere for eeeever and eeeever.'

Using emphasis

Try giving a different meaning to the following sentence by emphasizing a different word each time you read it 'Are you coming with me?' Emphasizing the important words in your talk will help the listener and add variety and colour to your voice.

You can enhance the quality of the word, e.g. 'I am *delighted* to hear your good news'; 'I was so *sorry* to hear he had died'.

With emphasis, you can put energy into your words. Try combining it with pausing. For example, 'He was (pause) a great leader'.

Further practice

I have mentioned the components of an interesting voice but reading about them will not improve your delivery.

You need to practise. If you do not have the opportunity to practise your speaking in public as much as you would like, or if you prefer to do so outside your own working environment, consider joining a speaking club which offers you the possibility of learning to present your views in an interesting and persuasive manner. At most of them, the members come from a variety of backgrounds with the common purpose of practising their speaking skills. Each speaker is assessed following his assignment, a prepared speech or spontaneous talk, say, so that he receives instant feedback on his performance to enable him to improve.

I advise my clients to read aloud. Try reading a book to your children, or read a passage from the newspaper into a tape recorder to learn how to add variety, colour and drama to your voice. To be a convincing speaker, you need the magical quality of enthusiasm. Although it may be bubbling away inside you, if your voice doesn't express it, your audience won't be able to share it with you.

Articulation – the clarity of the words

You should aim to make the consonants clear and precise – consonants carry the meaning of the language – vowels the sound. In order to make the consonants clear the organs making the consonant sounds must be clear and precise in their movements; the organs are: lips, tongue, soft palate, in combination with the teeth and hard palate.

Here are some useful exercises:

(a) Loosen jaw – draw hands down face and let jaw relax easily.

(b) Open and close mouth easily as you repeat FAH FAH FAH FAH. BLAH BLAH

(c) Loosening jaw –
SAH KAH SHE FAH RAH
PAH KAH SHE FAH RAH
WAH KAH SHE FAH RAH
BAH KAH SHE FAH RAH
DAH KAH SHE FAH RAH

(d) Loosening lips WWW WWW WWW BBB BBB BBB WBW WBW WBW.

(e) Loosening tongue – tongue tip to behind upper teeth and then to behind lower teeth (keep jaw open and still) LLD DDD LLL DDD LDL LDL LDL

(f) Combination loosening LLL LDL WWW LDL WLWD –

(g) Phrases for precise articulation:
   The tip of the tongue, the teeth and the lips.
   Lah lee loo lee. Zip e do da.
   Repetition, repetition, repetition.
   Whenever the weather is cold, whenever the weather is hot.
   We'll weather the weather whatever the weather whether we
   like it or not.

Variety in the voice can be achieved by variation in **volume**,
pitch, **speed** and **pause**.

   These exercises are designed to increase awareness of your
own speech rhythm and sound pattern. Speak them aloud,
varying your volume, pitch and speed.

Volume
Loud. louder. shout. quiet. quietest. whisper. silence.
Crash, bang, clatter, smash.   Hush, plush, slush.
Creep, peep, asleep.   Hit, bit, grit.

Pitch
Centre, high, low, deep, deepest, highest.
Up and down, awake, asleep, sky-high, ocean-deep.
When I sing the note gets higher and higher and higher.
When I speak the pitch gets lower and lower and lower.

In order to avoid a continuing downward inflection, don't start a
sentence on the finishing note of the previous sentence.

Speed
Fast, faster, fastest, quick, lightning, flash, slow, slower, cease.
Run, jump, leap, stop, slink, drawl, crawl, elongate, lengthen,
hiss, buzz, jab, insinuate, prod, glide, float, dream.
The lion gave a sudden stop.
He let the dainty morsel drop,
And slunk reluctant to his cage,
Snarling with disappointed rage.

Pause
Vary the time lapse between the following words:
Start.......stop..begin.end.........commence...
cease..go...stop.resume.............desist..continue..refrain

Reading aloud exercise

He came into the room, looked at the disorder and was perplexed. How it came to be like this he could not imagine. The silence was unbroken. He waited anxiously for some sign of life. Nothing at all. His eye moved furtively from wall to door, from floor to . . . corner . . . There in the corner, slumped between overturned chairs was a man, face drained to a pallor, and still as a lifeless creature. There was no phone in the house, no means of contact with the outside world. There was nothing to be done but to leave immediately and run, run as fast as he could away from the disorder, away from the chaos, away from responsibility. Tell no one, tell no one, get away, far away, run, run, fast, faster, faster: feet moving, feet, feet, feet, feet . . . out of step, not my step; step, other step, louder, nearer, quicker, thus, thud. Stop.

Summary – finding your voice

- Breath gives authority to your voice.
- Open your mouth for clarity.
- Vary the volume, speed and pitch.
- Silent pauses are powerful.

9 Practising and rehearsing

Mend your speech a little,
Lest it may mar your fortunes.
William Shakespeare

Is this really necessary?

There is no short cut to success and some experts in public speaking recommend one hour of preparation for every minute of presentation. Before you throw your hands up in horror, remember that this includes your planning, organizing and developing stages as well as the practice.

No one ever allows enough time to practise and some of my clients have a number of wonderful excuses why this should be so – the information for the presentation was only ready the night before – if I rehearse I get stale and I lack enthusiasm – I know the material inside out – I don't want to look too slick, and so on ad infinitum.

From my many years' experience of watching speakers, as well as from presenting my own speeches, I know that rehearsing helps you to:

- Become familiar with your material.
- Conquer the blank-mind syndrome.
- Feel more confident.
- Control nerves.
- Develop an effective speaking voice.
- Use positive and appropriate body language.

You are probably aware that practising is important and yet you keep putting it off until it is too late. I admit that I sometimes do the same and afterwards, when I have finished a presentation, I always wish that I had rehearsed more, because I know that I could have done it better. In reality, when we don't practise, we are using the audience as our rehearsal and that's not fair on them. We are not being fair on ourselves either. We've probably spent sufficient time planning the content and choosing the words, but we fail to allocate enough time to what will make the difference between a mediocre and a memorable talk – practice. Remember, if you can get up an hour earlier you gain an extra hour in which to practise.

One step at a time

There are three stages – practice, rehearsal and dress rehearsal. Practising is done by yourself, rehearsing in front of one or several people and a dress rehearsal is on site with props. All your practising and rehearsing should be spoken aloud.

How to practise

Your first run through will probably help you to add examples and even anecdotes which you hadn't thought of in your original preparation. I find that speaking, even to an empty room, frees the brain to be more creative and so, although I have a full talk prepared at my first practice, I stop and make notes and amendments. Also, if you are reading it aloud for the first time, you may find that some sentences are too long or complicated, your choice of words may sound clumsy or you may feel some ideas could be expressed more clearly. It's tempting to continue to alter words and phrases throughout your rehearsing. You must set yourself a time limit for changes, otherwise you will always be rehearsing new material and the main purpose of your practice, to become familiar with your talk, will never be achieved.

Don't forget your body language

You're practising to familiarize yourself with the ideas in your talk and words that convey them: you are also practising your body language and your voice.

Always stand when you are practising, so that you can use gestures and become used to holding your cards. Look around the room as if you were making eye contact with the audience. A full length mirror helps at this stage, although there is nothing to beat recording yourself on video. Don't dismiss this as impractical if you don't have your own camera. It is possible to hire one and, although not cheap, I think if you have an important business presentation to prepare, on which your reputation and that of your company rests, you should consider using video a worthwhile investment to help you improve your performance.

I know of one senior woman executive who changed her entire presentation after seeing herself on video because she realized that she was not conveying her message effectively. As she had begun practising well in advance of her 'performance' she had adequate time to do so; another reason for beginning your practice in plenty of time.

Using a tape recorder

If you can't video yourself, the next best thing is recording yourself on a tape recorder. Listen critically to your voice. Is it clear? Are you varying the pitch, volume and speed? Are you using powerful silent pauses or are you filling up the spaces with non-words? Above all, is there **enthusiasm** and **vitality** in your voice? Does it sound interesting? If not, analyse how you can improve it and practise again and again.

If you know that you will be addressing a large audience without the help of a microphone, place your tape recorder at the far side of the room and project your voice to it. Forget your inhibitions and your neighbours. Let them think that your behaviour is strange; it's more important that you practise now and get it right, than worry about the neighbours and later make a fool of yourself in front of 100 people. Make sure you are not straining your voice – remember if you have lungs full of air, your voice will carry further and you won't need to force it.

How to rehearse

At the stage where you can refine your presentation, a live audience is very useful. Use colleagues or friends, but be sure to give them the background to your talk – who the audience is, what they expect, what your objective is and what you hope to achieve. Only then can your rehearsal audience criticize your talk constructively. You will probably feel very self-conscious and embarrassed but don't give up, try to give your talk as if you had the proper audience in front of you. Make eye contact, use gestures and sound enthusiastic. Make sure they know that you want them to take the situation seriously and that it is important for you to have this opportunity to practise. Use your cards and if you lose your place, don't make any comment, simply continue as you would in front of a real audience; this will give you practice in overcoming fluffs. Encourage your rehearsal audience to ask questions as this will also be good practice for you. (See chapter on Questions and Answers.) They may want additional information on some aspect of your talk – if so, maybe your real audience would also benefit from a clearer explanation.

When you eventually receive their comments, accept them objectively. It's too easy to say 'Yes, but . . .' and make excuses for not listening to their views. Make notes of what is said to you and only look at them the following day, when there is less pressure on you and you can evaluate them dispassionately.

Remember that to profit from feedback you must accept criticism with an open mind. It may be irritating but consider what an oyster does with a grain of sand – you too can benefit from unpleasant criticism and use it to create a better talk. If you gather enough feedback, you'll end up with a valuable string of pearls.

Be sure to ask your audience to give you positive feedback as well. Not general praise, but specific instances of good performance – you need to know what to keep. In our courses, we insist that our tutors limit their recommendations to a maximum of three points at each feedback session otherwise the students are overwhelmed and unable to assimilate the training.

Guide lines for feedback

These are some questions which your rehearsal audience can use in order to assess whether or not you are presenting a successful talk. You may want to add some of your own which are more pertinent or relevant to your subject matter and objective. You can also use this check list to evaluate your own talk.

Introduction

- Is the first sentence attention grabbing?
- Have you shown the benefit to the audience in listening to you?
- Have you shown why you are qualified to speak on this subject?
- Have you announced your structure?
- Have you revealed understanding and knowledge of the listeners' attitudes and possible problems in the first minute or two?
- Have you identified with the audience early on?

Body of talk

- Have you announced your first point clearly?
- Have you used facts, examples, anecdotes, comparisons and statistics to support your main points?
- Have you summarized regularly?
- Have you recapped on the previous point before moving on to the next one?
- Have you used rhetorical questions to guide your audience along your path?
- Have you avoided jargon and abbreviations?
- Have you used visual aids in order to explain complex material or to add interest at a dull moment?
- Are the links between each point clear and logical?

Conclusion

- Have you indicated that the end of your talk is coming?
- Have you summarized your key points?
- Have you asked for action?
- Have you ended on a high note?

Check your timing

Always time every practice so that you know whether you need to add or amend your talk. If you overrun on time, don't follow what so many inexperienced speakers do – either ignore it and continue to the end of the talk or speak faster in order to include every precious point. Running over is a discourtesy to everyone and shows a lack of professionalism. Speaking faster means that your audience will not be able to follow and may stop listening. If you have too much material for the time **cut** or **condense**.

Write the timings on your cards, so that when you are delivering your talk, you will know how much time you have left at any given moment. This is particularly important with longer speeches or on the occasions when you have to deal with un-expected questions which use up the time allocated to your talk.

Look Mum, no cards!

As a final confidence booster, try giving your talk without your cards. Put them at the other end of the room and attempt a run through without them. If there are one or two stumbling blocks where you have to refer to them, do so, but continue again without them.

This will give you the opportunity to see the talk as an outline or as a series of ideas. If you can visualize the shape, it's often more helpful than trying to remember all the detail. After all it's probable that you know the subject well, so it's the sequence of points or the logical structure that you need to have at your finger tips.

Dress rehearsal

This takes place on the site and with the visual aids that you intend using. Most of what I want to say about this type of rehearsal is included in another chapter, Visiting the Site, but let me give you one or two suggestions about 'dress'.

Try practising at home in front of the mirror or on video with the clothes which you will be wearing for your presentation or talk. This is essential if your body language is to look natural. I have seen men and women casually try to put their hand in a pocket only to discover that their trousers or skirt are too tight and a relaxed gesture turns into a nervous struggle. Wearing the same clothes enables you to practise all your gestures and identify some of those which you may want to eliminate. I have a silk scarf which I love wearing, but because it keeps slipping, I tend to retie it repeatedly. Fortunately a co-trainer told me how distracting he found this, particularly when I was giving a lecture on distracting mannerisms. Now I only wear that scarf with a brooch securely pinning it so that it cannot move.

Watch out for fingers fiddling with rings, cuff-links, watches or constantly undoing jacket buttons. Keep your jacket fastened and don't fiddle with anything. Some men empty their pockets of everything in order to avoid fiddling, and this also helps to ensure their jacket sits smoothly. Wear the same shoes to practise in that you will for your talk. Are they comfortable, or are you likely to move from foot to foot because your shoes are pinching? Naturally you will make sure that your trousers have a sharp crease and your shoes are well polished. A speaker who stands in front of an audience in a badly ironed shirt, creased trousers and a jacket bulging over a large stomach does not help his presentation. A woman with a skirt that's a size too small, hair falling into her eyes and too much jewellery doesn't help her case either.

Summary on how to rehearse

- Make time to practise, aloud and standing up.
- Use gestures and vary your voice.
- Use a tape recorder and/or video camera.
- Practise in front of friends and colleagues and ask for feedback.

Remember you are the most important visual aid to your talk. Make sure that even before you open your mouth, the audience feels that you are an enthusiastic and interesting speaker.

10 Visiting the site

If you haven't struck oil in the first three minutes – stop boring.
George Jessel

I hope that this book will appeal to a wide range of readers. That poses a problem for me, however, when I try to cover all the speaking situations which different readers may be faced with. So I hope that you will select what is relevant for you in this chapter.

Even if your talks are always given to small groups in your own offices, don't be tempted to skip this section as I think you'll find it contains some hints and suggestions which will be new for you.

Where are you speaking?

Business talks are usually given in one of the following situations:

- Round-the-table meeting on your own premises, for example, union meeting, board meeting, sales meeting, departmental meeting, formal and informal.
- Clients/customer meeting in your offices or on their premises, generally a group of less than twelve.
- Regional meetings in hotels, such as a sales meeting with a medium sized audience.
- Conferences in hotels or conference centres with large audiences of over 150.

Visiting the site

Always attempt to visit the site where you will be talking allowing sufficient time to change or rectify any details which might prevent you from presenting well and efficiently. I know that this is not always possible, if, say, you are in Edinburgh and your client is in London, but even if you see the room ten minutes before the meeting is due to start, it will enable you to familiarize yourself with the layout and make minor changes. I am listing below the points which you should bear in mind when you are visiting a site.

Check list for small venues

- Ask yourself how you want the audience sitting; do they need tables? Would a semi-circle without tables facing the speaker be a better arrangement? Are there any members you want sitting together or separated or close to you? Can everyone see each other, you, and the screen (if you are using visual aids)?
- Is there adequate space for your notes, visual aids, handouts? Can you escape from the barrier of a table between you and the audience or will you be trapped behind it? Where will you position your flip chart and overhead projector?
- Where are the sockets for the equipment? Will you need an extension lead?
- How do you dim the lights if you are showing 35mm slides? Is a pointer available for you to identify details on the screen? How can you adjust the heating or air conditioning? Do the windows open?
- Who is providing tea/coffee and at what time? Imagine, your entire presentation could be jeopardized by the tea lady's appearance at a critical moment!
- Is there a clock in the room? Or should you take your own? It's often easier to read a small clock than your wrist watch, even if you remove it and place it in front of you.
- Who is providing pens, pads, drinking water?
- Is it to be a smoking or non-smoking meeting?

Check list for medium sized venue

- Check everything on the above list.
- If you are using a hotel, check the name of the manager in charge of hiring the room which you are to use.
- What time will you be able to get into the room?
- Who will be in charge and who will be on duty?

- Are the chairs comfortable? Can they be substituted by better ones if your meeting is long? Ensure that surplus chairs will be removed. Remember to provide a seating layout plan.
- Make sure that no telephones in the meeting room will ring and disturb you.
- Ask to see the visual aids equipment. Are you familiar with the overhead projector? Does it have a spare bulb built in or should you take one? Do you know how to focus this particular model? What type of screen will be provided? Do your own slides fit the projector? (See chapter on visual aids.)
- If you are using a lectern, how high is it? Can it be lowered or can they provide something for you to stand on if this is necessary? Does it have a light so that you can read your notes if the main lights are dimmed for 35mm slides to be shown?
- Are you operating your own visual aids and if not, what cues will you give to the projectionist?
- Check where the lighting switches are and who will operate them. Can only half the room be dimmed if necessary? Do the windows need to be covered?
- Where are the toilets and telephones; will you need a phonecard or loose change to make a call?
- What facilities does the hotel offer for taking messages?
- When and how will tea/coffee be served? Will it be served in the meeting room or in an adjacent room? If it is in the same room, ensure that the cups are laid out prior to the commencement of the meeting. You don't want to give your talk to the accompaniment of rattling china.

Check list for large conferences

Here most of the details should be organized by the conference co-ordinator. If that happens to be you, I suggest you buy another book, because I can't list here everything you need to know. As a speaker your responsibility is to consider every aspect of your own talk and how you can ensure that your presentation will be professional and trouble free. Here are some points to consider:

- How will you approach the platform/stage?
- Where will you stand?

- Will there be other people on the stage with you?
- Is there a teleprompt?
- Can you see the audience or are the lights shining into your eyes?
- How are the visuals cued up?
- What type of microphone is provided? Is it fixed or will you be able to move around?
- Is the text of your talk being distributed to delegates and if so, when?

Dress rehearsal for small groups

Once again you may feel that for a small group presentation, a dress rehearsal is not necessary – I urge you to stand in the spot where you will be speaking and at least once, rehearse out loud. This is particularly important if you are using visual aids, as you want to be sure that all the equipment works and that you feel confident using it.

In a small room, you should sit in all the seats to ensure the screen is visible from all positions. If possible, ask someone to take your place as speaker so that you can check that you will not be obscuring the screen when you are addressing the group. I often find in such a group that I have to stand to one side when a visual is showing so that I am not in the way (read the Chapter on Visual Aids for more information on this). While rehearsing, move from the flip chart to the overhead projector and across the area that is your 'stage' and check that no cables or junction boxes are in your path.

While you are rehearsing, remember to re-time your talk on site and allow sufficient time for your audience to absorb the information contained in your visual aids. In a small group, there is a greater likelihood of interruptions and questions from your audience during your talk and therefore I suggest you plan to talk for five minutes less than your allocated slot so that you keep within the time limit.

Theatre style

Classroom style

Discussion style

Meeting style

Classroom style

Workshop groups

Informal discussion

Seating diagrams

Dress rehearsals for team presentations to clients

If you find it difficult to rehearse by yourself, it will take even greater discipline and courage to insist that those who are jointly presenting with you should rehearse as a team. I know how easy it is to outline roughly what each of you will do and casually reassure each other that it will be fine on the day. This is a big mistake. You should all have a very clear idea of exactly what part of the presentation you will be covering, as well as how you will hand over to each other and whether one member can supply additional information if someone else omits it. I have seen terrible glares directed at someone who thought she was being helpful when she chipped in with an important point which the speaker had apparently forgotten. This kind of team support can be invaluable, but be sure to arrange between yourselves how it is to be handled, otherwise it can cause bad feeling. Make sure everyone understands their role and the framework in which they are speaking. This may sound too formal to you, but it can be handled in a manner which appears relaxed and casual and allows everyone to be sure of what is expected of them.

I remember an unsuccessful presentation I made with another consultant at the beginning of my career in which he misinterpreted a sign from me and continued talking on all the points which I was expecting to cover, thus resulting in a rather unbalanced presentation. We had been reluctant to rehearse together and we were sure we knew our stuff – we did, but we hadn't presented as a team before.

If you are working as part of a team, ensure that you have anticipated questions and planned answers as well as which member of the team should give them. In a sales presentation where your prospective clients are judging your company, a united team will go a long way to convincing them that you represent a reliable and successful company.

Dress rehearsal for a medium-sized group

As the visual back-up becomes more elaborate and includes additional people, your technical dress rehearsal is even more important. You may not be in direct control of the visuals and the projectionist will be relying on you for a voice cue or a light cue (you press a button which flashes a light next to the projectionist).

Your dress rehearsal should start at the point where you are first visible to the audience. Rehearse your entrance as well as stepping on to the platform. I remember seeing a woman in a tight skirt struggling to get on to the stage. This didn't make a good first impression. Some forethought could have prevented that. When you are introduced, walk purposefully to your speaking spot, pause, look at the audience, make eye contact and give them your 'I am happy' expression, take a good breath and then start to speak. That silence may feel long to you but it allows the audience to focus on you and begin to listen. It shows them that you are in control. Novice speakers often start to speak too quickly and deliver in a high and rapid voice which lacks credibility and loses the audience's attention immediately.

Dress rehearsal for a large audience

One of the most difficult performances I have ever given was in a large conference centre where half a dozen people were scattered about talking to one another and paying no attention to me. Occasionally doors opened and new people came in or shouted out obscure messages. Lights dimmed or suddenly brightened for no apparent reason and visuals flashed on and off the screen. Through all this, I gave my presentation. Well, if you haven't guessed it already, I was at a dress rehearsal.

Very often they are disorganized but you should make the most of them because every moment of practice will help you to give a professional performance. Take the opportunity of practising your entrance as well as your introduction and your entire talk complete with cued visuals. If you are using an auto cue for the first time, you will need some additional tuition – it is a knack to be able to use it well but in order to be effective, you must practise several times. Don't rely on one dress rehearsal to get it right (see chapter on Reading a Script).

Familiarity breeds confidence

These are probably the most important three words in this book and if you only follow this advice, you will become a better speaker.

Most of our worries about speaking in public are based on the fear that we will make a fool of ourselves, or worries about what people will think of us. We want the audience to respond and react and our biggest fear is that they won't. In fact it is unlikely that the audience will fail to respond, but in order to realize this, we need confidence.

Unfortunately you can't conjure confidence out of the air; it will only come with practice. Your audience will believe in you if you believe in yourself. Practising gives you confidence and enthusiasm – a winning formula.

Summary of visiting the site

- Always visit the site however small.
- Double check everything (if something can go wrong – it will).
- Rehearse on site.
- Re-time everything.

11 Relaxation exercises

In this chapter I am going to describe some techniques for relaxing, which you can practise at any time you are feeling tense, as well as in the final moment before you begin to speak.

Why is relaxing important?

If you can relax the tension in your muscles, you'll find that your voice will sound more sincere, your gestures will look natural and you will use fewer non-words and fillers. As you learn to control your nerves and feel more confident, your muscles will relax automatically, but here are some exercises to help you in the process.

Getting into the habit

I once attended a seminar on hypnotism and was selected by the hypnotist as a guinea pig. He taught me how to self-hypnotize so that when I found myself in a minor panic about being late for an appointment, I could park the car and sit for sixty seconds and allow myself to go into a mild trance. Then I would arrive in a more relaxed frame of mind. Unfortunately, I failed to keep practising this technique and I'm not able to use it any more, but I have retained the memory of how my body feels when it's untensed. Some people don't have that awareness. 'What do you mean relaxed – I *am* relaxed!' they say through clenched teeth.

In order to learn how to relax, you must first feel the tension. Start with your toes and curl them up as tight as possible, hold this position for 30 seconds and then release. Next tense your calf muscles, hold for 30 seconds and release; tense your thigh muscles and buttocks, hold for 30 seconds and release; tense your stomach and chest, hold for 30 seconds and release; tense your shoulders and neck, hold for 30 seconds and release; tense your face, hold and release. There is no need to rush this exercise – do it slowly to get the maximum benefit.

You can practise it before you fall asleep at night and you'll feel a warm tingly feeling all over your body. By being aware of the contrast between your tensed and relaxed muscles, you'll get into the habit of being able to relax at will. You'll simply recognize your tension and tell your body to let go. It's impossible to be relaxed and anxious at the same time. This exercise will only work for you in moments of high stress (like speaking to an audience) if you have practised it sufficiently in un-stressed moments.

Learning to be centred

This is fundamental to performing. An uncentred performer on the stage looks like an amateur and an uncentred speaker inevitably feels tense. Your centre, your 'point of power', is situated roughly at the solar plexus, above the navel. To help you to be centred, try this exercise: Stand straight, bend your knees slightly, close your eyes and concentrate on your feet. Feel each toe digging into the floor as though you were curling your toes in sand. Now squat, keeping your feet flat on the floor. Imagine that your legs are pillars of iron connected to the centre of the Earth. Rest your hands on your knees for balance. Stay there until you can feel your centre of gravity lowering to your pelvis. Rise slowly, straighten up and breathe.

This exercise also helps with your posture: stand sideways before a full length mirror and bend your knees slightly. Notice how your pelvis and buttocks are out of alignment with your back. Now place your hands on your hips and gently roll your pelvis forward, pulling your stomach in and down. Your buttocks should now be aligned directly under your back in a straight line. Now imagine a string running all the way up your spine and out of the top of your head. Let the string hold you like a puppet. This exercise centres you and enables you to use natural and graceful movements.

Five minutes to go and in private

Be a rag doll   Allow your body to flop down from the waist and swing your arms like a rag doll. If no one can hear you, say 'I don't care – I don't care – I don't care' as you hang loosely. This will get rid of the tension in your upper body.

Shoulders on parade   Pull your shoulders right up to your ears and let go; repeat this exercise five times to release the tension in your neck and shoulders.

Roll your shoulders backwards four times and roll them forwards four times.

Roll your head over your right shoulder, let it hang backwards and then bring it round over your left shoulder and finally rest your chin on your chest. Reverse the direction and repeat four times. This exercise helps to relax throat and neck muscles.

Wibbly wobbly   Shake your hand from your wrist and then your arm from your shoulder and finally let all your upper body shake, including your head and lips.

Horse laugh   Loosen your lips and blow through them like a horse.

Facial exercises   Stretch your lips into a silent E and purse them into a silent O and now rapidly say a silent E, O, E, O. Repeat ten times. This is an excellent exercise to release the muscles around the mouth which can make you look severe when you are feeling nervous.

Yawn   In the chapter on Voice, I have described how to make yourself yawn at will. This will relax your neck, throat and mouth area.

One minute to go and in public

Tense all your muscles (not your face this time) and release. Repeat twice.

Breathe deeply and exhale fully. Concentrate on your rhythmic slow deep breathing.

Be curious about your surroundings and your audience. See how many red ties you can count. If you are in a small group, look at everyone's suit and note the different patterns in the fabrics.

Think of a peaceful scene – walking through a pine forest – lying on a warm beach – the view from a hill across several green fields on an autumn afternoon – feel a deep inner stillness and quiet confidence.

Think positive thoughts and you will be a success.

12 Understanding your audience

To sway an audience, you must watch them as you speak.
C. Kent Wright

I've said earlier that anyone who is listening to you is your audience, but obviously a large group of people behave differently from a group of five or six sitting informally in your office.

We know that no one listens with total concentration and that they can be distracted by you, the speaker, as well as by their own internal thoughts. Now I'd like you to consider the dynamics of the group and the interaction between the different members. I have divided up this section according to the size of the audience, i.e. small, medium and large as the techniques vary for handling different groups.

1 Speaking to small groups

The interaction with a small group (1–15) is often visible.

You should be aware that in a meeting of several tiers of authority, i.e. managing director, marketing director and marketing manager, each person will be interpreting your message at two levels – his own, and how he imagines his boss and/or subordinates are receiving it. You have probably been in the situation where you have a good working relationship with one or two people and find that they act differently when joined by other colleagues. This is normal and shouldn't affect your presentation or talk. When I am making a presentation to, say, a board of directors, where I am friendly with one or two members, I speak with the same degree of formality to all of them as it would be inappropriate for me to reveal our friendship.

You should bear in mind the personalities and relationships which exist within a group when you are presenting your ideas. Remember to maintain eye contact with everyone; it can be tempting to only look at a friendly face or at the most senior member whom you wish to impress and avoid looking at someone who you feel may disagree with you. Try to treat everyone in the same way.

Discover personal barriers and relationships

Within your own company you will be aware of conflicts or liaisons which exist between people. Meetings with other companies, where you are not so familiar with the internal politics, can be more difficult. Use any contacts you already have to learn about the men and women who will be your audience. It can be helpful to know of any quirks and personal likes and dislikes. For instance, the style of dress which is considered appropriate for a business presentation depends on the culture of the organization. One of my clients, a creative and artistic film director failed to obtain financial backing for a project because of his colourful shirt and casual suit. His bank manager didn't think he was serious enough to justify a loan. I know of one senior executive who cannot tolerate speakers who use a cover to reveal slowly the contents of a visual aid on an overhead projector. He won't allow any of his staff to use this method as he considers it an insult to the audience and feels that the speaker is playing games with them. An outsider to this company could easily antagonize him without being aware of the reason.

Find out as much as you can about the audience so that your message will be accepted and not rejected by their own personal barriers. Speaking to an unknown audience can be like crossing a minefield but if you do your research you should be able to pick your way through and deliver an effective talk.

If audience research is impossible, you can set aside the first few minutes of your presentation to ask questions about them and their situation. All good sales people know the importance of listening and this is your opportunity to practise this skill; their answers will help you tailor your material to their needs. I am not suggesting that you should change the core of your talk, but you can use the audience's own problems and experiences as examples.

Speakeasy training always allows for the participants to introduce themselves at the beginning of the course. I remember during one of our courses, a student told me her talks had been criticized for lacking structure so when we reached this stage in the training, I checked with her personally that what we were suggesting would help her in the planning of future talks.

Find out:

- Who will be there.
- Their position and power.
- Relationship with each other.
- Attitude to your company and product/service.
- Previous knowledge and experience of the subject of your talk.

Interpreting their body language and responding to it

In the chapter on Body Language I emphasize the importance of eye contact, because an audience will stop listening if they feel you are not interested in them – looking at them shows that you are.

Watching the faces of your audience has another important advantage – it enables you to see how they are receiving what you are saying. In a small group this is particularly important because you can react to them. If someone is looking puzzled, you can check that they have understood: 'Gerald, would you like me to expand on that point?' Someone may nod in agreement and you can involve them by saying 'Margaret, you look as if you have had some experience of that yourself'.

By placing their name at the beginning of your question, you alert them to the fact that you are talking directly to them and they can either decline or accept your invitation to speak. Be careful not to look surprised or disappointed if they don't respond, but simply continue with your talk. By speaking directly to them, you have involved them and shown your willingness to include them.

When someone is looking bored or uninterested, you can also ask them a question to allow them to express their thoughts, but if they do not answer, try not to be distracted by their lack of interest. For instance, I hate to see someone smothering a yawn, although I suppose an open yawn is worse. However, I have learnt to ignore it now; because although it may indicate boredom, it could also be totally unconnected with my talk and have arisen through a sleepness night due to a sick child, a late night party or even a sign to the rest of the audience that the 'yawner' is superior and wants to distance herself from the meeting.

The non-verbal interaction between the members of the audience can also show you how your message is being received. Watch out for eye contact between them as well as nods of agreement or negative signs like a shake of a head. Facial expression reveals much of what a person is thinking and feeling, but you should also pay attention to their bodies. Sitting forward indicates more interest than sitting back.

You may feel that delivering a talk is difficult enough without closely watching and interpreting body language. In actual fact, I am sure that you are aware of all these signs already, but you may not have realized how you can use them to become a more effective speaker. Audiences want to feel they are important to the speaker and by acknowledging the signs which they are giving you (sometimes unconsciously) you are paying them a compliment. (See also chapter on Persuading, Convincing and Selling).

Other involving techniques

Presenting to a small group is a challenge because you are addressing individuals. You do need to break up your monologue to include them occasionally.

You can interpret their thoughts by watching their body language and involve them by directing a question to someone who may have a personal contribution. 'John, I believe you've had experience of this in your department, could you tell us a little about it?' Or 'Shirley, what particular problems have you come up against using the old system?'

In this way, you not only enliven your talk with real-life examples, but you also give the audience another voice to listen to, which will help to extend their concentration span and allow you to speak for longer.

Remember to build 'comprehension questions' into your talk, so that you can check their understanding: 'Would you like me to expand on the last two points before I go on to the next?' Listen carefully to any comments or questions but confine your answers to the material you have already presented and don't be tempted to reveal part of the rest of your talk. If you use 'comprehension questions' you will be involving the audience, checking their understanding, but remaining in control of the situation.

How to cope with interruptions from the small audience

So much for the techniques of involving your audience, but what do you do when the audience involves itself by interrupting?

'Above all remember that you should be in control and not allow the audience to take over.'

How can you deal with them? Try to remember that you are in charge, that it is your show and that you should control what happens.

Let us imagine that you are in full flow and a member of the audience asks a very relevant question. It is up to you to decide how to handle the situation. If you feel that you can respond and continue with your talk without a falter, do so. However, many speakers are distracted by questions and find it difficult to resume their flow if they stop. If you are one of these, I suggest you lay down some ground rules before you begin speaking. Suggest that you would like to take questions at the end, but if anyone has difficulty following your talk, they should ask you to explain more fully.

The main advantages of keeping in control and not letting people interrupt you is that you stick to your predetermined structure, which you have designed to enable the audience to follow easily a logical sequence of points. Even if *you* have no problem in presenting your material in a haphazard manner in order to answer questions as they occur, your audience will be confused and may find it difficult to follow.

The chapter on Questions and Answers deals more fully with handling questions, but I think you should be aware at this stage of the reasons why people ask questions.

Often it's because they want more information or don't understand a particular point. They may, however, see it as an opportunity to be controversial or witty in front of their boss or subordinates. If you suspect that this is the case, answer politely but don't allow yourself to be drawn into an argument or a discussion. You can remind the questioner that you have not finished your presentation and that you would like to return to his question at the end.

You may find yourself in a position of being unable to say 'I'll answer that later'. If your boss asks you a question in the middle of your presentation, you may feel obliged to answer it. Do so using the minimum number of words and tell her you find it easier to present the whole talk so that she can see it in its entirety. I have seen a one-hour meeting spread over the whole afternoon because the speakers allowed themselves to be interrupted.

Remember the concentration span of your audience is limited and if you don't keep control their minds will wander and your ideas will not be accepted or even remembered.

2 Speaking to medium-sized audiences

You will find that a group of more than twenty people has a different character from a smaller group as each member loses some individuality and takes on the identity of the group. As a speaker your eye contact is more general and therefore the audience feels less involved; they may feel that there is less need for them to concentrate because they are less visible.

Think of how you feel in a group of five, of fifteen, of fifty and of one hundred and fifty and you will see how an increased number of people changes the quality of the audience.

Interaction with the medium-sized audience

I consider a group of twenty to thirty as a medium-sized audience and you'll realize that you can't have the same personal inter-action with each member as you could with a smaller group. Although you should certainly be aware of the audience's body language, you can only address that which appears to be most common – one person looking puzzled can be ignored (unless she is the most senior executive present) but half a dozen indicates that further explanations are necessary.

How to control the audience

It is more important with a larger group to keep control as there is a greater potential for disorganization if you allow yourself to be side-tracked by spontaneous questions and comments. Do let them know that you want to keep interruptions to the minimum and provided that you smile when you say this, no one will take offence; if you tell them how valuable you know their time to be and that you don't want to waste it, you should find that they will co-operate.

Should you sit or stand?

Always stand if you possibly can. In some companies there is a tradition that speakers stay sitting and it takes a brave soul to break the convention. Try to be that brave soul. You will feel awkward and self-conscious to start with, but you will look and sound more powerful. Explain that you want to stand so that everyone can see you and that your voice carries better.

You should not rest your hands on the table in front of you but should stand tall and confidently project your voice to the furthest person (to overcome the sound of air conditioning, people coughing and shuffling papers, etc.) and maintain eye contact with as many people as possible. Remember to push your chair well back or even stand behind it and make sure your briefcase or handbag is not in the way of your feet. If possible stand without barriers – table or desk – between you and your audience. Your path to the flip chart or other visual aids should be clear and if your handouts are to be distributed during the talk, ensure that they are in two or three central locations, so that this can be accomplished quickly and with little disruption.

To give a professional presentation and achieve your objectives, you must consider every small detail because you want the audience's attention focused on your talk and not on some minor distraction. Take a few minutes before you begin to speak to check the area around your feet for any obstacles and to check the space you have for hand and arm gestures; enthusiastic gestures are very effective provided they don't knock somebody on the head.

Include everyone with eye contact. By varying your gaze, you can avoid the Tennis Game effect – right, left; right, left.

3 Speaking to large audiences

When you can't see the whites of their eyes, you're addressing a large audience and entering the realm of public speaking. Individual eye contact is impossible except for those people in the first few rows, but you still need to look in the direction of as many people as possible. Remember to include other speakers and the chairman who may be on the platform with you. Your body language should be more exaggerated and in particular be sure to smile more than in a smaller group as a person at the back of a big hall will be able to discern a proper smile but will not see a small movement such as a raised eyebrow; a friendly expression is going to be more effective even when talking at a serious business conference.

Researching 200 people

You need to research a large audience as much as a smaller group. If you are speaking within your own company, you'll have no problem finding out what you need to know. However, if you are addressing a large group who have come independently to a public conference you will need to address your questions to the organizers. Find out:

- How and why the audience is coming?
- What was written in the announcement of the conference?
- Who else will be speaking and on what aspect of the topic?

I like to contact the other speakers by telephone to check that I will not overlap with their material. Also, if another woman is appearing, I ask what colour she'll be wearing in order that my choice of outfit doesn't clash on the platform.

It always surprises me to see how speakers fail to chat to their audience at coffee breaks and meal times. I find these times an invaluable source of material and will often refer to a conversation which I have had with a member of the audience prior to my talk. For example, 'Someone was telling me during the coffee break that . . .' and this leads into my next point. It has the advantage of showing the audience that you are approachable and that you can relate to their problems and experiences. And you benefit from speaking face to face with the individuals who are your audience. It is also more relaxing than trying to fit in a final mental rehearsal.

Prepare for interruptions

In a formal conference, there are fewer interruptions. However, you should plan how you would deal with the odd question which may come in the middle of your speech.

Using common identity in large audiences

As a general rule it is more difficult to maintain a high degree of attention with a larger audience, because they are more likely to be distracted by their own thoughts and you can't use as much personal involvement. So take advantage of the fact that they will act as a group in many instances. Laughter is infectious and an amusing story which might only raise a smile when told to an individual will get a more significant response from a larger audience. Humour is also a great unifier and if you can use it to relax the audience, they will appreciate you as a speaker. In large groups, if you can appeal to their common hopes and fears, their shared experiences, their admiration and contempt, they will respond to you.

Understanding their concentration span

Audiences can only concentrate on one speaker for a limited period of time, after which they listen less attentively and eventually become fidgety and bored. The concentration span depends on a number of factors:

- Their initial interest in the subject.
- The time of day – people tend to be most attentive first thing in the morning and least attentive after lunch, particularly if they have been drinking alcohol. This period is known, by speakers, as the Graveyard Slot.
- Whether or not they think the speaker will expect them to answer a question.
- Their own opinion and assessment of the speaker.
- Their need to know about the subject.

Generally, an audience will concentrate most during the first ten minutes of the talk and their interest will remain on a low plateau until they hear the words 'Finally let me conclude by saying . . .' From this you can see that you need to state your main message strongly at the beginning of the talk and repeat it at the end.

Ideally, one speaker should not talk for more than twenty minutes. I know that in many situations this is not practical, so I suggest a maximum of forty minutes. If you need to speak for a longer period, I advise you to consider splitting the time slot between two speakers. Be sure to work closely with one another, rehearse together, and remember to plan ahead of time how you will deal with questions, so that you can give a united perform-ance.

How to use interest prompts

There is frequently a low period in the middle of the concentra-tion span and it's up to you to include interest prompts in your talk to keep the audience's attention.

Interest prompts can be:

1 A change of position – move from behind a lectern to centre stage; and in a smaller room, move from a flip chart to stand closer to one of the listeners. If you have been sitting, stand; and vice versa. In an informal setting, consider perching on the edge of a table in order to vary your position.

2 Use a visual aid – be careful not to use a visual aid only as an interest prompt (see chapter on Visual Aids). Write on the flip chart or use a slide on the overhead projector or pass round a sample.

3 Do something unexpected – take off your shoe and bang it on the desk to make your point.

4 Involve the audience by asking a question.

(a) Rhetorical – the listeners will be prompted to give a mental response, e.g. 'Where can we find the solution to this prob-lem?'
(b) General question answered by a show of hands: 'Who has installed a new computer system in the last year? Put up your hands.'

(c) General question answered by one or two people with a direct answer: 'Who here can give me the details of a problem that they have encountered?'

(d) Direct question: 'Mr Smith, what did you do when the fire destroyed all your records?'

Except for (a) above, always wait for an answer; remember the audience needs time to adjust from passive listening to active participation, so don't be afraid of the silence.

5 Involve the audience in action.

(a) Ask them to work out a calculation, using their own situation as a base and applying the theory which you have just presented.

(b) Ask the small/medium audience to move to a demonstration table to see a model in action and, better still, get involved in some way.

(c) Ask for a volunteer to write on the flip chart.

(d) Ask them to turn to the person sitting next to them and discuss a point raised in your talk.

You'll see in the chapter on Preparation and Planning that your talk should include several interest prompts at various points to add variety.

Other ways of preventing boredom

During the coffee breaks, if possible, open all windows to get a change of air, particularly if you have a smoky atmosphere.

You can ask people to stand and stretch.

I had to speak in the Graveyard Spot, i.e. after lunch, at a conference in a hotel venue, with no windows and to an audience of approximately a hundred business men who had been sitting all the morning and had indulged in a good lunch. What a challenge! As I was addressing them on the importance of presentation skills, I decided to emphasize breathing and voice projection and asked them to join me in several exercises. After a reluctant start, they all participated and no one had an opportunity of going to sleep.

I have seen the third speaker in a long evening's presentation ask the audience to stand and move about on the spot to get rid of 'dead bums' before she began her talk.

Formal business presentations with senior executives may not be the place to practise some of these techniques, but do be aware that as the speaker, you are in control of the audience. If their concentration is lagging, your objectives will not be achieved and your talk will not be remembered.

Summary – understanding your audience

- Research your audience.
- Watch their body language.
- Use comprehension questions in small groups.
- Control the interruptions.
- Use interest prompts.

13 Questions and answers

Be sincere; be brief; be seated.
Franklin D. Roosevelt

Whenever you talk, your audience will want to ask questions, therefore it is prudent to anticipate how you'll handle them.

When to allow questions

In a small group you may decide to allow questions throughout your presentation as they will occur naturally when they are most relevant and you will be in a good position to control them. It's always a good idea to encourage questions if you are presenting an instructional talk as you'll need to check comprehension – and questions can provide valuable feedback for you.

I have said earlier in this book that I prefer to ask for questions to be kept until the end of my talk so that I can present my material in the order which I have chosen, but when I am running training classes, I often pause for questions so that the monotony of one voice is broken. This helps to maintain a higher level of concentration and allows the listeners occasionally to become active participants; questions also enable me to check that everyone has understood.

There are disadvantages to allowing questions during your presentation:

- They disrupt the flow and structure of your talk.
- The answer may be contained later on in your talk.
- Only one person may be interested, i.e. the questioner.

You may be able to manage a spontaneous question and answer session in a small informal group, but large audiences need to be controlled more firmly. If you are the sole speaker, let the audience know when you expect questions and even suggest to them that they jot down those which occur to them as you are talking.

You should always schedule your questions before your final summing up so that you can end on a positive note. Don't forget that your last words to the audience will be retained longest and you don't want these to be a minor argument which you had with a questioner. When question time is over, if you have been unlucky enough to face any difficult or hostile questions, you should regain control by repeating your main points. Demonstrate to the audience that you are a reasonable person by finishing on a humorous note if this is appropriate.

When you restate your main proposition, include any comments from the audience which support it and ignore adverse questions or remarks. Thus, you show that you are confident and can cope calmly with controversy. The audience doesn't want to see you embarrassed and they expect you to behave in a professional manner.

If you are introduced by a chairman, be sure to check with him beforehand who will handle the question and answer session. Unless you are part of a panel discussion, my personal preference is for the speaker to control the questions.

Questions to a panel

On a panel it's advisable to allow questions immediately after each speaker, because if the audience has to wait until all the speakers have spoken, they will probably only be able to think of questions for the final speaker while the rest of the panel sit there looking superfluous. This happened to me at a conference where not a single question was directed to me, as I had spoken after lunch and the panel discussion was scheduled for the late afternoon. When the Chairman finally took pity on me and redirected a question, I was unable to answer as it was not within my field of experience. The panel questions are valuable provided that the individual speakers have also had the opportunity to answer questions directly after their own talk.

How to encourage questions

- Tell the audience when you expect questions, i.e. during or at the end of your talk.
- Ask them to jot down questions during the talk.
- Allow them enough time, at least ten seconds, to change gear from being passive listeners to active participants.
- Plant a colleague in the audience to ask a question.
- Ask one yourself, such as 'You may be wondering why my company has come to specialize in this area; let me tell you . . .' 'I am sometimes asked about my personal background and you may be interested to know . . .'
- Ask the audience a question. 'Did anyone disagree with the area of my talk dealing with the advertising budget, as I know that it is a contentious issue' or 'By a show of hands, could you indicate how many of you have used our services in the past?' And then direct a question to someone: 'Would you care to tell us of your experience, Sir?'

Too often speakers cannot tolerate the silence which follows when they ask for questions and they don't allow sufficient time for the audience to respond. Your body language should be alert and interested but you can indicate that you consider the ball to be in their court by leaning back, maybe sipping some water and adopting a non-threatening listening stance. Above all, don't look anxious.

Rehearsing questions and answers

The question and answer session should also be rehearsed. There are some obvious advantages; practising helps you to:

- Handle the unexpected.
- Anticipate questions.
- Field difficult questions.
- Highlight weaknesses in your argument.
- Expose ambiguity.
- Answer questions using additional data.

How to rehearse

When you are closely involved with a subject, it's possible to arrive at a point where you are talking in your own shorthand and not fully explaining the logic of your arguments. This can be a particular danger when you are an expert talking to a 'lay' audience. Rehearsing your talk in front of colleagues and friends and asking them to probe any areas which are not completely clear will help you to avoid this pitfall. If your actual audience has a high level of technical knowledge, try to find someone with a similar degree of understanding of the subject with whom you can rehearse.

When questions arise during your rehearsal period, analyse them and the reason why they have been posed. Is the question:

- Relevant.
- Referring to material which appears later in your talk.
- One which you want to practise answering for the question and answer session.

Ask yourself whether these questions have arisen because of a lack of clarity, too much detail, an illogical argument or simply because it is impossible to include everything and such a question can be answered at the end of your talk.

Often you can hint in your talk that you will explain further if anyone asks you to do so at the end of your talk. 'As you know we decided not to increase our exports to the USA this year and if anyone would like me to explain further on the reasons for this, please ask me at the end of my presentation.'

When you have discovered most of the areas which you think may provoke questions, prepare your answers carefully, including additional research into data which you may not have had time for in your talk. You will feel more confident if you know that you have fresh supplementary material to support your case. Be sure to take it with you in a form which is easily accessible during what may be a stressful time. You don't want to be seen shuffling through several files in your briefcase muttering 'I am sure I had it here somewhere . . .' If you are speaking to a small group, consider preparing an extra handout which outlines the additional evidence.

Look back to your ideas map and re-evaluate some of the points which you had to reject because of time constraints – might they form the basis of a question and answer session?

You may have omitted complex financial figures or technical analyses from your talk as they were inappropriate for the audience. But you may have to anticipate a question which requires you to provide more exact information.

How to answer questions

Many inexperienced speakers find it difficult or impossible to handle questions because they fail to do one simple thing – they fail to listen to the question. So remember these points:

- Listen to the question – be sure that you understand it and if not, ask the questioner to repeat or explain it.
- Make notes of the main points of the question.
- Ask for the questioner's name (and company if it's a public meeting), so that you can refer to them by name.
- Restate the question – this helps you and the rest of the audience to know what question you intend to answer.
- Answer it concisely – give your answer directly and if necessary supply statistics or use an illustration or even a personal experience to support it. Your audience has heard your speech, so don't give them another; make sure your answer is succinct.

Some don'ts

- Don't be defensive – it's easy to feel that the questioner is your adversary, particularly when your subject is controversial. Be calm and polite as you acknowledge the questioner 'I am sure that many people will be glad you asked that question . . .'
- Don't rush to answer the question – allow a pause as you consider the full implication of the question and how you can best answer it.
- Don't bluff – if you don't know the answer, say so (more on this later).

'Don't be defensive – it's easy to feel that the questioner in the audience is your adversary, particularly when your subject is controversial.'

- Don't embarrass the questioner: 'I've already answered that but you obviously weren't listening.' Instead say something like 'I'm sorry I didn't explain that clearly'.
- Don't get into a dialogue with one questioner. If she insists on asking a supplementary question, answer it briefly and then break eye contact. Look towards the other side of the room or

hall and indicate that there is another question. Suggest that
as there are several more questioners, you could discuss her
question in more detail after your talk. If a senior manager is
monopolizing question time, you can ask him if you could
answer other questioners and return to him afterwards.
Remember you should aim to stay in control of the situation.
(Also see How to Stop Ramblers.)

■ Don't answer questions which aren't relevant or interesting to
the audience. I have witnessed a tax expert who was giving
general information on taxation for small businesses become
embroiled in a detailed question from one member of the
audience. He should have suggested that it was inappropriate
to discuss one individual case, instead of attempting to
answer a personal question which was more suitable for a
private discussion.

What to say if you don't know the answer

No one likes to admit their ignorance and if you are the expert
having just presented a successful talk, it is even more difficult. I
am afraid you are going to have to bite the bullet. To help you,
imagine that there is someone in the audience who is longing to
expose your weakness. So far your presentation has been excellent but suddenly he hears you giving wrong information – you
are bluffing – up he jumps, at last he has caught you!

So what can you do if you can't answer a question? Simply
admit you don't know, and say you will find out and give the
questioner the information when you have had time to do the
necessary research. (If it is a public meeting, ask her to leave her
name and telephone number with the Chairman.) Sometimes
you can use the audience. Ask if anyone has had experience
which could help the questioner. You can learn a great deal from
the audience, and occasionally it won't be necessary to admit you
don't know the answer.

I had a client recently whose boss delighted in throwing
impossible questions at him at their monthly departmental meeting. My client was made to feel inadequate in front of his staff as
he attempted to answer. We advised him to face his boss and ask

him what questions he needed to prepare for the meeting. This worked for a time until an unexpected question came flying across the room, but fortunately he felt courageous enough to say he didn't know as he hadn't prepared and that it required a detailed answer as it was such an expert question. From then on our client's boss seemed to have fewer questions.

How to answer difficult questions

Hypothetical questions They are generally prefixed with the words 'what if . . .' 'So what happens if the new budget isn't approved?' Don't let yourself be drawn into 'doomsday' situations. Instead answer: 'We've spent two months preparing the new budget. It's a good budget and we're confident we'll get approval to put it into practice.' Politicians generally refuse to answer such questions and you can follow their example by saying that there is too much supposition in the question for you to give a sound answer.

Leading/loaded questions 'Surely you can see how unfair it is for the staff if we close the canteen during August? Why are you insisting on this?' If you don't challenge this first statement, it will appear that you agree with it. 'Everyone knows that this company is making vast profits, so what we want to know is why can't the typing pool have one more typewriter so that the work can be completed faster?' Remember once again to correct the first statement before you answer the question. 'I'd like to know why you think this company is making vast profits.' Here is another example: 'We know that you have found it difficult as the only woman on the board, dear, but do you feel you have achieved anything in your first year?' Don't be tempted to rise to the bait by saying 'Yes, I have found it very difficult and principally due to your pompous chauvinistic attitude.' Instead you need to change the word difficult. 'Before I answer your question, may I just correct you on one point. I wouldn't describe my first year as difficult. I have found it stimulating and challenging, but above all very enjoyable.'

Off the record questions Don't be fooled into thinking because you are addressing a small friendly group, you can speak candidly and in confidence. Answer all the questions 'on the record'.

The yes or no questions This can appear to be very aggressive. 'Just answer yes or no. Is the pay increase agreed or not?' You don't have to limit your answer to yes or no – respond in your own words. 'I have considered the proposal for a pay increase from three angles and I think you should know what they are. First . . .'

'No win' questions 'Can you explain the decline in the sales – is it due to poor management or poor selling?' Don't feel you must answer such a question with an 'either'/'or' answer. You could say: 'I prefer not to see it in such black and white terms as there are a number of important contributory factors.'

Useful phrases

The cliché 'I am glad you asked me that' enables you to gain thinking time and you should develop a few more original phrases to help you organize your thoughts before and even during your answer. Here are some suggestions:

- 'To help me answer your question more accurately, could you tell me exactly why you are asking it?'
- 'I can see that you feel strongly about that and I admire you for saying so.'

Sometimes you will not want to answer a question, so you should think of how you can deflect it:

- 'We have spent some time on that problem/question, but what I think is more relevant to consider now is . . .'
- 'There is some merit in those points and it has been useful to hear from you but perhaps you are not aware that . . .'

How to stop ramblers

On occasions, you'll find that a questioner is unable to pose a question successfully and instead presents a long-winded rambling speech. What can you do?

- Use body language – hold up your hand and indicate that you want to answer the question if there is one. If not, simply give a brisk thank you and move on to another questioner.
- Highlight one part of the ramble and re-phrase it in order to give a short answer.
- Use your voice to interrupt while explaining that time is running out and you can see that there are several other people who wish to ask questions.

Your body language during question time

Remember that your positive confident stance shouldn't disappear when you stop talking and start taking questions. Listen intently to the question, even if you think the questioner has totally failed to understand your argument, nod encouragingly and look pleasant.

As you begin to answer the questioner, look at him directly. However, if it's a fairly involved reply, look around and make eye contact with the rest of the audience and include them in your comments. You can also use expressions like 'I know this applies to many of you . . .' or 'I expect you'll find this useful . . .' so that they don't feel excluded. If you see that some people are nodding or appear to want more explanation, you can extend your answer after asking 'I can see several of you nodding; is this a problem that some of you have had to tackle already?'

If you feel under attack, don't allow your body language to reveal your unease – continue to look pleasant and confident as you search in your mind for suitable counter-arguments. At a meeting recently, I saw a colleague being given a tough grilling so that afterwards he felt thoroughly exhausted. When I commented on how he had appeared confident and in total control, he said 'But you couldn't see my pounding heart'. He was right and so don't let yours show – remember people take you at face value – so keep looking poised.

Summary – questions and answers

- Announce when you will answer questions, i.e. during or at the end of your talk.
- Plan a technique to encourage questions.
- Rehearse questions and answers.
- Don't bluff – admit ignorance.
- Use positive, pleasant body language.

14 Making and using visual aids

A picture is worth a thousand words – or is it?

In this chapter I am going to explain the advantages and dis-advantages of the most commonly used visual aids as well as describe how to design and make visuals which will enhance your talk or presentation.

Why use visuals?

The objective of most business presentations is to inform or persuade or a combination of both, but information which is received by listening is retained for less time than that which is received by seeing. Therefore visual aids help to make your talk memorable. They also help to explain complex ideas in a form which is easily understood; relationships and comparisons can be shown more clearly in a visual format; statistics, figures and financial data in general are more digestible and comprehensible when presented visually.

Visuals can reinforce an idea which you have already discussed in words; for instance you could outline a cost-saving theory and then show visually what the actual savings would be in practice.

Remember that visuals can add interest and spice to the dull patches in your talk as well as humour.

Effective visuals should be used to:

- Help the audience to retain information.
- Save you time in explaining concepts, ideas, etc.
- Avoid misunderstandings.
- Reinforce ideas.
- Add spice and humour.

Do you need visuals?

Speakers often regard visuals as the magic ingredient which will turn a turgid talk into a professional presentation. In fact I have seen more good talks ruined by inappropriate visuals than I have seen poor talks improved by good ones. Even when the visuals are good, the speaker often finds it difficult to incorporate them smoothly so that they, and the speaker's behaviour, only distract the audience. So make sure your visual is *an aid* and not a distraction and make sure your aid is *visual*.

Beware of adding visuals to your presentation for the wrong reasons; they can be costly, difficult to use and confusing for the audience. One speaker I know uses them as a prompt. He has most of his key points on overhead slides and refers to them throughout his talk. What an insult to the audience! He is ignoring all the advantages of talking to a live audience and suffering all the disadvantages of reading. Your audience can be reminded of your key points after you have spoken them, so use a visual to summarize but not as a prompt.

Don't add visuals because the other speakers are doing so. Your talk may not need them.

Don't use visuals to brighten up an uninteresting talk – improve your talk and only use a visual to illustrate it more vividly.

When to use visuals?

To show an idea visually. On page 20 you will see a sketch of an ideas map. This concept has been described in the text of the chapter on Preparation, but I think you'll agree that by seeing an example it is easier to understand. During my courses I always use an overhead projector transparency to demonstrate the ideas map as it saves time in my explanation and also shows the class how it looks. Any discussion of techniques or methods can benefit from a visual illustrating how they work in practice. Cut-away drawings of machinery or tools can be very helpful on practical, instructional courses.

Figures are difficult to understand when spoken. Comparisons can be made more easily when they are displayed visually. Here is a pie chart showing the relative importance of three factors to consider when speaking. These figures appeared in the text of a previous chapter, but I think you'll agree they make more impression when portrayed as shown in the illustration.

Speakers' impact

Why use a visual?

Ask yourself why you are using a visual. Is it to:

- Present facts, concepts, figures, in a comparative or structured form?
- Aid comprehension and prevent misunderstanding?
- Reinforce your message?
- Focus your listeners' attention?
- Maintain interest and help retention?
- Motivate the audience to make a decision?
- Add humour?

How to choose a suitable visual

Once you have decided that your talk would benefit from the inclusion of some visual material, choosing the method to display it can be difficult. On the table (see pages 168–9) showing the advantages and disadvantages of the various types of visual aid, you'll see that not one of them is perfect. However here are some of the considerations for you to bear in mind, when selecting a visual style:

Available equipment Most companies have an overhead projector and flip chart but if you are presenting a talk on your client's premises, check the size of their projector, as you don't want to lose half an inch from the edge of all your transparencies. Audio visual equipment is available to hire in most large cities but if you are using hired equipment, don't try to save money by only ordering it for the day of your talk. Make sure you can rehearse with it at least one day in advance and for more complex presentations with several speakers, ensure that you have it for two or three days before the actual presentation. Hotel equipment varies from excellent to appalling, so make sure you see it beforehand in order to check its suitability for your talk. I have run courses throughout the country and I am amazed that some hotels which offer 'Conference Facilities' can be so unaware of what is needed by speakers.

Size of audience If the audience can't see what's on the visual, you are likely to antagonize them and lose their attention. Certain aids aren't suitable for groups of more than thirty people, i.e. flip chart, blackboard, whiteboard. This is a rough estimate and the size and layout of the room may allow you to increase or decrease that number. If you are presenting to a small group of five to six people, don't dismiss the idea of visuals as inappropriate; a large screen is not always necessary as you can easily project overhead projector transparencies or 35mm slides on to a blank wall.

Size and layout of room Long, narrow rooms with poor lighting are not suitable for the smaller aids such as flip charts. Sometimes conference facilities offered by older hotels are located in rooms with pillars or asymmetric walls which can make it difficult to set up a screen which is visible to all the audience. If you are sitting on a platform you may have to re-arrange the speakers' chairs so that they don't obstruct the screen.

Lighting If you are using 35mm slides make sure you can darken the room. Some offices don't have blinds at the windows and I have come across hotel rooms with curtains which are decorative but not functional. Overhead projector transparencies can be shown in natural light but occasionally you will need to block out sunlight if it is shining directly on to the screen. Avoid shadows on the flip chart if possible and don't place it against a window or another source of bright light as this will make it difficult to read.

Seating arrangements Make sure you arrange the seating so that everyone has a clear view of the screen. Sometimes this is difficult with older-style projectors which block some of the audience's view. In the seating diagrams on p. 103 you will see that the position of the projector and screen can usually be adjusted so that it's visible to everyone.

Cost versus frequency of use Transparencies for the overhead projector can be made easily in the office, either manually, with a photocopier or by using a computer with the right software. These transparencies are adequate for an internal meeting but for sales presentations to clients or large conferences, consider using a slide production company. If you are using slides repeatedly, i.e. a road show travelling round the country or for training and teaching purposes, it's worthwhile having your slides or transparencies professionally produced.

How to look professional when using visual aids

1 Flip charts

Always carry your own marker pens as they can dry out quickly and those supplied may not write well; also you can be sure that you have the right thickness and colour for your purpose.

You can prepare the flip chart in advance but if the paper is thin, only write on every other page, otherwise some of your audience will attempt to decipher what is written on the next page. Use block capitals in a variety of colours to ensure that your visual is easy to read and attractive to look at. Remember to cover your prepared flip chart until it is relevant so that it creates maximum impact. Flip chart pads are usually 25" × 32" but they are also available in larger sizes and a smaller variety for use with desk top easels. If you are drawing graphs or working out calculations seek out paper which is printed with faint squares – they are invisible to the audience but make it easier to write in a straight line.

The height of some easels is adjustable. I remember seeing a short speaker struggling with a large piece of flip chart paper trying to fold it over against a strong current from an air conditioning duct. Practise turning the pages over and if there is any difficulty lower the easel or arrange for one of your listeners to help you at the appropriate time.

Use a paper-clip or fold over the corner of the page to indicate your next visual or a visual to which you want to refer back during the course of your talk.

Flip charts are not suitable for large audiences so their use is limited to informal groups of approximately thirty people, and are used most effectively during the course of a presentation to note information given by members of the audience, to calculate, or to highlight and summarize essential points. In my classes, as I conclude each of the points outlined in the chapter on Preparation and Planning, I write them on the flip chart. This serves as a visual reminder of the point I have reached in my talk and, because I have previously announced my structure, if a listener becomes distracted he can tune back in by glancing at the flip chart. Your main points on the flip chart can help you to summarize at the end of your talk. Consider using two flip charts so that one can display the key ideas while the other is used as a scribbling pad.

I have seen a speaker at an internal meeting open her talk with a question to the audience 'Now what do you think are the chief factors we need to consider about our new timetable?' As the audience responded she noted their points on the flip chart and addressed each in turn. You must be sure that you can anticipate what your listeners will say if you employ this method and you must also show why you are not accepting some of their answers; for example, 'I'm not going to write down Holiday Schedules because we will be discussing this in more detail at the meeting which is planned for Friday afternoon.' If you genuinely want a contribution from the listeners, it's important that your body language indicates this. Stand relaxed, but ready to write, making encouraging eye contact with each of them.

Using a flip chart in brainstorming sessions is helpful as it enables all the points to be visible to your group. As each sheet is completed you can tear it off and stick it on to the walls around the room so that there is a complete picture.

Some speakers are reluctant to make use of the flip chart in front of the audience or during the course of their talk because they fear they won't be able to write clearly or, worst of all, their spelling will let them down. Use lined paper to overcome the first difficulty and bad spellers can always admit their weakness and ask for help from the audience. If you can anticipate some of the words which you'll need to write, note them in pencil at the side of the flip chart; your audience won't be able to see them and you'll have a crib to refer to. If you are using the flip chart to summarize your main points, prepare it in pencil to be certain of correct spacing of your letters and words. In a later section, you will find hints and pitfalls to avoid in preparing the contents of your visuals, but if you make a mistake while preparing your flip chart you can either tear off the sheet and start again or paste paper over the error, wait till it dries and write on it. Limit your use of paste or you'll find your pages will stick together.

Writing clearly and quickly on the flip chart in front of an audience is not easy and if you're planning to use it frequently, I suggest you find time to practise as it's a skill which can be learnt.

Hints on using the flip chart

- Stand to one side of the easel, on the left if you're right handed and on the right if you're left handed so that as you write you are not obstructing the audience's view; this position allows you to glance over your shoulder occasionally, to keep eye contact with your listeners. Also stand to one side of the easel if you are indicating points of the flip chart.
- Don't hang on to the easel for support.
- Never write and speak at the same time. This is one of the

most difficult rules to follow but remember that anything that
you say while you are writing will not be heard by your
listeners. There are two reasons for this – firstly they will be
concentrating on what you're writing and not listening,
secondly your voice will be muffled as it will be directed to the
flip chart and not to your audience.

■ Don't hold a marker pen in your hand when you're not
writing.

■ Look at the audience and not at the flip chart. Speakers break
this rule more often than any other because eye contact with
the audience is difficult and looking at a familiar flip chart is
comforting. Learn to overcome this problem and face your
audience.

2 The overhead projector

This is probably the most versatile form of visual aid as it is
suitable for large and small audiences, slides are easy to make and
projectors are universally available. The smaller desk version is
easy to carry to locations which don't have suitable equipment.
Unfortunately, overhead projectors are also the most commonly
misused form of visual aid and often distract both the speaker and
the audience.

The equipment consists of a simple box with a transparent top.
The light source is a bulb in the box and translucent or transparent
material is placed on the box top and projected on to a screen by
means of a lens and mirror system mounted directly above it.

Use it as a scribbling pad

Most overhead projectors are used to project transparencies on to
a screen but when a roll of acetate film covers the transparent top
it can be used in a similar manner to a flip chart, i.e. to note down
audience contributions, to summarize decisions, to show calculations or to use as a scribbling block for the speaker to illustrate
visually theories and suppositions.

You can use pre-drawn diagrams or outlines and then complete
them in front of the audience while explaining the significance of
the additional material. Alternatively you can place an incom-

1 Projection head. Tilt head or mirror to position image on screen
2 Platen. Always remove dust before a presentation
3 Focus adjustment
4 Transparency locating pins*
5 Lamp brightness switch*
6 Lamp on-off switch
7 Spare lamp control*
8 Lamp height adjustment*

*Not always fitted

An overhead projector

plete transparency under the acetate roll and draw on the finishing lines without marking the transparency which you may want to use on another occasion.

As the speaker sits alongside the projector facing the audience, he can continue to make eye contact as he writes, which he can't do while using the flip chart. This secondary use of the overhead projector is generally more suited to lectures and informal training sessions.

Understanding the Equipment

In order to get the most out of using the overhead projector, you should be familiar with each piece of the equipment:

The screen Try to match the screen size to the size of the audience and place it at least two screen widths from the front row and not more than five from the back row. Place it across a corner of the room rather than in the centre of a wall (see page 103 for the seating diagram), make sure the top of the screen can be tilted forward towards the projector to avoid the keystone effect (this is when the top of projected transparency is wider than the bottom – if it's not possible to adjust the screen, place something under the front of the projector to raise it). Bright lights and sunlight shining on the screen will mar the picture, so make arrangements to avoid this.

The projector Very often projectors are placed on trolleys which fit them snugly but leave no space on which to put the transparencies. Try to find a low table with adequate room for the projector and the transparencies and hopefully you will be able to project sufficiently high so that the top arm of the projector doesn't interfere with the audience's view. When the equipment is set up, sit in every seat to check that there is an unobstructed view of the screen. When the transparencies are being projected you may need to step to one side to avoid blocking the screen. If you are using the continuous roll of acetate as a scribbling block or to note down your summaries, remember to place a low chair next to the projector or you may end up squatting and attempting to write while not falling over. Get a colleague to check visibility when you are alongside the projector.

Transparencies Place a transparency on the projector and aim to fill the screen avoiding an uneven white border of light. You may have to move the projector backwards or forwards to adjust the picture size. Turn the knob on the vertical column to adjust the focus. If the projected image has brown corners, this is an indication that the bulb support should be raised or lowered and this can be achieved with the lamp brightness switch (see illustration).

The bulb Some projectors are designed to carry a spare bulb which is easily slipped into place by moving a small lever on the front of the projector.

Hints on using the overhead projector

- Never switch on the projector unless your transparency is in place. A blank bright screen attracts everyone's eyes. If you doubt this, stand in front of a group and switch on the projector without a transparency. You will see all eyes focused on the screen and until you project a visual, everyone's mind will be in a state of anticipation for what is to come. The impact of your visual is lost if you place it on the projector after switching on.
- Always switch off the projector before removing your transparency. The speaker who waves her transparency over the projector is providing a minor distraction and a blank screen is unpleasant to look at.
- Allow sufficient time for your audience to absorb the content of your transparency. I am often amazed that speakers who have obviously spent considerable time on producing excellent transparencies leave them on view for such a short time. Remember, they may be very familiar to you, but the audience is seeing them for the first time and requires an adequate period to understand their full significance.
- Don't talk while the visual is showing (or at least allow a few moments of silence when you first switch on the projector). The reason for this is that the sense of sight is more powerful than the sense of hearing (one of the advantages of using visual aids), so your listeners will be looking and not listening.

It's difficult to remain silent but if you look at the audience and wait until most of them have returned their gaze to you, you will know when to recommence speaking.

- Explain the visual. This is not always necessary but it may speed up the audience's comprehension; certainly the main point of the visual should be repeated to help to reinforce it.

- Point at the transparency and not at the screen. I have seen a speaker standing on tiptoe and apologize for not being able to reach the furthest corner of the screen to indicate some vital statistic, when all he had to do was to point at the transparency on the projector.

- Use a pen not your hand. A hovering, possibly shaky finger over the transparency will be magnified on the screen so place a pen or pencil (with a flat side to prevent it rolling off) on the projector to mark the relevant area.

- Never look at the screen after placing the transparency on the projector. You are allowed to look *once* over your shoulder at the screen to ensure that it is correctly lined up. I cannot count the number of speakers, many of them professionals who should know better, who find the screen has a magnetism which forces them to keep looking at it. I have even seen speakers continue to look at the screen after they have switched off the projector. One of the main strengths of the overhead projector is that you can use it with normal lighting and that you can continue to face the audience. Keep looking at them even when their attention is on the screen and while you are explaining the details of the transparency. So what happens if you suddenly get a blank mind and can't remember what is shining out behind you? Look at the projector. The transparency is showing the correct way up and is a duplication of what is on the screen. Remember that no one will be persuaded by the back of your head – they need to see your face all the time.

- Never walk between the projector and the screen. You will lose authority as your transparency is projected on to your face and the light will dazzle you.

- Remove the visual as soon as it is no longer relevant. Once you have moved on to another point, switch off the projector immediately and remove the transparency, otherwise it becomes a distraction. You can partially reveal information on the visual by placing a piece of paper under the transparency to cover the material which you don't want to show. By sliding the paper down as you pass on to new points you can expose more of the transparency. I suggest placing the paper *under* and not over the transparency as this allows you to move it further down without the paper falling off.

3 35mm slides

If you have recollections from the past of noisy projectors which often stuck and were difficult to load, you will be happy to know that this type of equipment has improved enormously. Be sure to insist on having a modern projector with remote control and if this is not available arrange for it to be hired. 35mm slides are the best method of adding visual aids to your talk in a professional manner. They are not as flexible as overhead projector transparencies because, once the carousel is loaded, it is impossible to change the order or omit slides during your talk. However, you can project 35mm slides more quickly and more smoothly.

They have the disadvantage of needing a darkened room, making it difficult for the audience to take notes or for the speaker to see the audience; you should arrange for a spotlight to shine on you during the slide showing so that your listeners can see you and also to help you read your notes. Because of the need to change the lighting your slides should not be sprinkled throughout your talk but shown together in one section. Slides are suitable for larger conferences and you should consider whether a production company, who could organize the whole event, with a set, sound equipment, lighting and several projectors would provide a more polished and professional finish to your show.

If you are arranging your own meeting or conference using 35mm slides, here is some of the equipment which you will need:

The screen Place the screen in the centre of the room and use a remote control to change slides. If this is not available you will need to work in close harmony with the projectionist to indicate the moment to move from one slide to another. For informal groups, you may choose to project the slides on to a suitable blank wall.

The projector Place the projector directly in front of the screen, making sure that it doesn't obstruct the audience's view. The focus is generally located on the front of the projector around the lens and you should ensure that you have a spare bulb and sufficient extension cable to reach the socket. Consider using two projectors to avoid the unprofessional blank screen at the point where the slide changes over. A twin dissolved unit adds a final efficient touch to any presentation, and can be hired at a relatively low cost.

Slides The content of the slides is described later on, but remember that a carousel holds 80 slides so try to avoid having 85. Have your slides mounted professionally in hinged cases with glass which can be easy cleaned. These ensure that the slide stays in focus whereas the cheaper type tends to move in the projector.

The carousel When you load your slides, stand by the carousel, looking towards the front of the room, following the beam of the projector's light, hold the slide above the tray in a position so that you can read it. Place the slide in the carousel upside down, so that the top of the slide enters first. Many speakers make the mistake of turning the slide over before loading and this causes it to be projected back to front.

Hints on using 35mm slides

- Number all your slides and make sure your script is marked so that you know where each should appear.
- Double check that the carousel is correctly loaded.
- Practise your entire presentation at least twice, with the projectionist or by using remote control.
- Mark on the floor the exact position of the projector in case it is moved after the rehearsal.
- Don't look at the screen; talk to the audience.

- Don't talk while the audience is preoccupied with an interesting slide.
- Leave the slide on for sufficient time to enable the audience to absorb it and remove it as soon as it's no longer relevant.
- Use a plain colour slide, the company logo or the conference slogan between slides; never show an empty screen.
- Don't move between the screen and the projector while it is on.
- Use a pointer to indicate particular areas of interest, but put it down when not in use and resist the temptation to use it as a walking stick, or to conduct the audience like an orchestra.

How to design effective visuals

Most of what I'm including in this section applies to both transparencies and slides. However, some of the basic rules regarding simplicity and clarity are also applicable to prepared flip charts. Even if you have an in-house audio visual department or if you intend to use an outside agency, you should have a comprehensive idea of what makes a successful visual, as they will need to follow your instructions.

Don't use verbal visuals

There are two rules regarding visual aids:

1 Don't put any words on your visual.
2 Very occasionally break the first rule.

Words don't make good visuals, but unfortunately, many speakers consider that their listeners will be unable to follow a talk without a script in front of them. The greatest insult of all is to start your presentation with a visual proclaiming 'Good Morning' or 'Sales Presentation for Mr New Business'. These words should be spoken, not written. Words on a visual encourage your listeners to become readers and while they are readers, they can't be listeners.

Verbal visuals are a distraction as members of your audience will be reading at different speeds and if you attempt to read the slide for them, most of them will have finished before you anyway.

A sales manager recently showed me a typical verbal visual which looked like the illustration below.

Sales strategy

Key accounts
- Closer liaison with senior personnel
- Frequent visits by representatives
- Special terms and conditions

New business
- Analysis of existing customers
- Telephone sales to targeted groups
- Direct mail for new products
- Exhibitions throughout the country

This speaker displayed his visual and then proceeded to talk about each point. You may have seen and possibly used many visuals like this one and you may feel that it is effective, so I'd like to explain why it is not only a poor visual, but a positive distraction.

In assessing a visual, you need to ask yourself what is its purpose? What does it add to the presentation? Why is it there? The purpose of the visual above is to tell the audience of the main points in the speaker's talk. He doesn't need a visual for this. What does it add to the presentation? The speaker may feel that it reminds the audience of what he is talking about. He should be doing that, not a visual. Why is it there? So that the speaker can use it as a prompt? He should use cards for this.

This visual is a liability because by showing it, the speaker relinquishes control of the audience. He should be carefully leading them along the path he has chosen for them by revealing each of his points at his own speed. With this visual he reveals everything so that there can be no sustained interest and no element of surprise. On the contrary, he has given the audience the opportunity to disappear down Route 350 as they mentally debate the implications and the likely outcome of each of his points.

You may think that, because I have suggested announcing your structure at the beginning of your talk, you will have lost the element of surprise anyway. This is not true. When you outline your structure, you simply show the steps you'll be taking to reach a particular goal without giving details. Our sales manager could announce his structure by saying 'I'm going to talk about our sales strategy and I'm going to tackle it from two angles – key accounts and new business'. No doubt at this point some speakers would like to flash on the screen:

Sales strategy

* * Key accounts * *

* * New business * *

However, consider a more creative picture showing a sketch of major customers sitting on pound signs alongside new customers with question marks over their heads stretching into the distance. The style could be light-hearted or serious, depending on whether you use cartoon characters or stick men and women.

You may want to use a visual to remind your audience about the content of your talk, but you should be doing this verbally by recapping after each point; if necessary, you can use the visual to summarize. Our sales manager could say 'So I have identified key accounts as the first step in our sales strategy and here again are the main areas which I think we should tackle.' His visual would look like the illustration below.

Key accounts

■ Closer liaison with senior personnel
■ Frequent visits by representatives
■ Special terms and conditions

How to use words in visuals

Try to avoid using words on visual aids but if you need to, limit their use to identification (i.e. labelling diagrams), recapping and summarizing.

Remember that any words which you include on your visuals must be legible from the seats furthest from the screen. Letters on an overhead transparency must be at least a quarter of an inch (6mm) high and the larger the better. Use a uniform typeface throughout and always write words horizontally, even in pie charts or when identifying machinery parts which may be positioned at an angle.

Here are some other considerations for designing effective visuals:

Keep them simple Many visuals are ineffective because they are complicated and contain too much information. They are difficult to understand and therefore become a distraction. You may need to separate out material in order to present it on several slides; analyse what is the most significant data and reject the rest. Remember that round figures are easier to understand, i.e. £1 million is more comprehensible than £1,103,284.83. If you are preparing a series of transparencies showing the information in stages, you could, for example, start with a graph showing the sales targets and overlay a second transparency with the actual sales figures; with 35mm build-up slides you can add information to each slide; for instance, a map of Great Britain could be filled in with the regional sales figures. This method allows you to remain in control of the speed at which your audience assimilates information and also allows you to explain any inconsistencies or anomalies in the data. For instance, the sales manager might add this, 'You will notice that sales figures for Scotland appear to have increased at a faster rate than those for the rest of the country, but bear in mind that International Mechanics, one of our larger customers, moved to Aberdeen in January and so their sales are included in Scotland now'.

Tables of figures rarely make good visuals, as they often contain too much information and they can become very complicated to read. Pie charts and bar charts are often a simpler method for relaying data. If you have no alternative but to show a table of figures, do remember to highlight in colour the figures which are pertinent to your presentation to ensure that your audience is concentrating on the right column.

Keep them uniform I have found that clients who previously considered that a few typed notes on acetate was an adequate visual aid, will sometimes go to the opposite extreme after some tuition on the merits of creative visuals, and use the flip chart extensively in between showing a number of highly coloured transparencies and 35mm slides. Don't use too many types of visual and don't attempt to make them too diverse. A jumble of typefaces and styles and a mixture of colours gives the impression that the speaker and his company are disorganized and confused. Choose a clear simple typeface and use it throughout your slides with a bold background colour to create a smart effect.

Keep them colourful Judicial use of colour can significantly enhance your visuals as you can use it as a background or to highlight important data. Don't include one black and white slide if the rest are coloured as it will lack impact. Even overlaying with tinted film can improve the appearance. Use colour to underline and for bullet points and arrows. Remember to aim for a contrast, for instance light letters on a dark background. However, remember that some colours lose their intensity when they are projected. Always avoid white letters on a yellow background or vice versa and pink on red, as they become invisible. You can use a primary background colour to indicate the various sections of your talk, i.e. the sales manager could use blue on the slides when illustrating his section on key accounts, and change to red when he moved on to new business.

Keep them humorous If you can introduce an element of humour into a serious presentation, you will be revealing the fun side of your character which will warm your audience to you. Beware of being flippant, but cartoons can add a light touch to dry material which will help maintain your listeners' interest.

Visual styles

Pie charts

A pie chart is a circle divided into 'slices' which visually indicates the relative value of each slice to the whole (see illustration at the beginning of this chapter). It is a very useful type of visual as it's easy to produce and suitable for technical and non-technical audiences. Use as few sectors as possible and never exceed five or six. The most important sector should be placed at the 12 o'clock position and if all the components are of equal value, arrange them from the smallest to the largest or vice versa.

Sectors can be coloured or highlighted to indicate their importance but be sure that any lettering or figures will show up over the background colour. Sometimes it's preferable to identify the sectors by means of arrows positioned at the side of the pie. Remember always to place your words horizontally; don't follow the shape of the pie.

Bar charts

Pie charts are useful to compare fractions within a single whole, but bar charts can be used to highlight the relationship between two variables, e.g. age and salary or productivity in geographical areas, as well as to illustrate trends and make comparisons. They should be simple and easy to follow, so when designing them, you must identify the relevant information and discard the rest, or present it as a second or third visual.

Bar charts can be drawn vertically or horizontally, but the former are more appropriate to indicate a time element and when one item has to be shown several times, e.g. annual sales figures for the last five years. The time scale is normally shown along the bottom line.

Horizontal bar charts have two advantages, firstly the information can be presented in any sequence, e.g., sales figures for the month of July can be shown alphabetically by the rep's name or by geographical area or in order of size or even randomly; secondly there is more space to identify each bar. Remember that the labels can be placed at either end of each bar or even below and above them.

Sliding bar charts are used to show a sub-division within a total, e.g. each bar showing sales figures could be sub-divided into sales for existing customers and sales from new customers. Using different colours for each division gives them more impact.

Line charts and graphs

These can be used instead of vertical bar charts and are particularly useful when a greater number of time periods needs to be illustrated; for instance, a three-year sales period with monthly totals would require 36 bars which would be difficult to represent clearly. Line charts or graphs are also useful to illustrate minor variations in data, which would not be noticeable with bar charts. Variations can be highlighted by using a broken scale which does not begin at zero, but with the amount where the minor variation appears; e.g. if the monthly sales figures over a twelve month period ranged between £40,000 and £45,000 per month, the scale ranges from £35,000 to £55,000 in order to emphasize the variations. Be sure that the broken scale is clearly marked otherwise the audience will assume that it starts at zero.

Flow and organization charts

Flow charts illustrate the stages of development in a process or the passage of documents through a system, and organization charts show the functional relationships and flow within a group or company. Both are useful to demonstrate visually links and connections which might be difficult to understand and remember without a chart.

Tables of figures

These should be interpreted in a visual manner. However, if due to budgeting or time constraints this isn't possible, consider highlighting the key figures. Use a coloured pen to ring the relevant data so that the audience concentrates on it immediately and doesn't get drawn into reading the rest of the table. Block out

line graph

broken scales

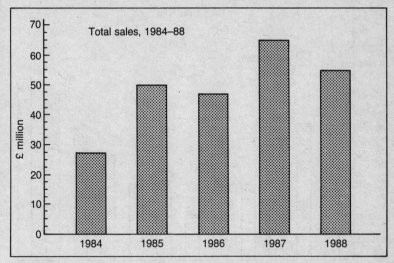

Total sales, 1984–88

bar charts

Sales by region, July
£ thousand

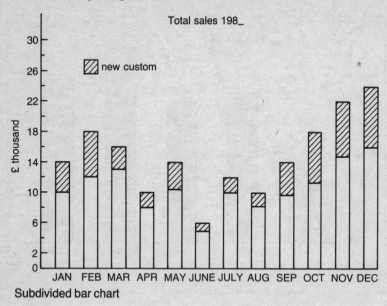

Subdivided bar chart

the irrelevant information if you can. Remember that the figures on their own are insignificant without analysis, so don't leave the audience to puzzle over their meaning. Avoid using the following on your visual:

- Computer printouts.
- Typewritten material.
- Tables of figures.
- Forms.
- Printed material from books, newspapers, articles.

Financial and technical presentations usually suffer from too much detail. This is particularly noticeable when expert speakers are addressing lay audiences. If you are in this position, make sure that your audience research is thorough, enabling you to put yourself in their shoes. Stand back and isolate the most important features and ignore the qualifying elements which may be fascinating to you because you are so closely involved with the subject. Aim to make your visuals simple and not cluttered by unnecessary detail.

Be original

This chapter has been devoted to the traditional methods of adding a visual element to your talk. But don't limit yourself. Be original. I saw a stimulating use of some very ordinary props during a presentation by a chairman to his staff on the company's gross profit. '£8 million sounds a lot of money, but what happens to it?' He proceeded to take a jug of orange juice and pour it into a number of glasses which he had set up on the table. 'So much has to go on wages and salaries', he said, filling up one glass. 'We must allow this much for National Insurance Contributions and PAYE', he said, as he moved on to the next glass. He proceeded to fill the rest of the glasses (he had marked the correct level for each one before he began his talk), with the overheads of the company. Eventually, he was left with a small amount of orange juice in the jug. 'This is what's left', he said and measured it into the remaining two glasses. 'Just enough to pay Corporation Tax and dividends to the shareholders.' He held up the empty jug, 'So much for our profit.'

He had explained the financial situation to a non-financial audience in a manner which was easy to understand. Try to find new and simple methods of explaining complex material.

Hints on using a production company

The range of services which are offered by production companies is vast and your choice will probably be dictated by your budget. You can use them to produce well-designed transparencies for the overhead projector and 35mm slides only, or you can hand over the entire organization of your sales conference including guest speakers and participants from around the world. This book doesn't aim to show you how to run a large-scale conference. However, I am including some suggestions for using outside assistance which may help you to avoid some of the common pitfalls.

Advance planning Contact the professionals as early as possible. If you are planning a large conference in a major city, contact them even before you have decided the date, they may be able to help with your choice of venue.

Ask questions   The professionals may talk in jargon and abbreviations but don't be put off by that. If you don't understand what they are talking about, ask.

Allow sufficient time   You will naturally want to include the latest sales figures or the most recent data in your presentation, but don't make this an excuse for not providing the production company with scripts in plenty of time. If necessary you can add the final figures later, but at least you can avoid the expense of having their staff working over weekends and evenings in order to prepare many last-minute visuals.

Late changes cost money   Nothing is impossible, but everything costs money. Ensure that everyone, and that includes the Chairman, has prepared a script which won't need eleventh-hour changes. Remember that slides will be prepared to illustrate certain points in the script and if the words are changed, the visual may have to be scrapped.

Summary

- Make sure you really need your visuals and that you're using them for the right reason.
- Make them simple, colourful, consistent and relevant.
- They should visually aid your talk and not distract from it with verbal printouts.

Note: The rest of this chapter is reprinted, with permission, from *How to Make Overhead Projector Transparencies* © 3M United Kingdom plc 1982

Although both vertical and horizontal formats are acceptable, the horizontal is usually considered best for audience viewing. Remember these points:

1 Titles should generally be at the top of the original.

2 Information should be in the upper two thirds for better visibility.

3 Have a focal point, the point of interest, in the centre of the transparency.

Creating good visuals

An overhead projection presentation is only as good as its visuals, and the visuals are only as good as the originals. When you can't find original material that's right for your needs, you'll have to make your own. Here are three essential points to bear in mind before you begin:

1 Visibility

Write, print and type large and legibly on every original. Letters should be at least ¼ inch (6mm) high. If the original can be read from 10ft (3m), it will project well.

2 Clarity

Every element on a visual should be instantly recognizable. If it isn't, label it. Use colour for clarity and emphasis.

3 Simplicity

Limit each original to one point or comparison. Break paragraphs into sentences, sentences into words.

Image area and size

Nothing is more frustrating than spending valuable time producing an exciting visual original and then finding that it's bigger than the image area available. Follow these points and you won't get frustrated:

1 Limit your image area to 7.5 inches by 9 inches (19cm by 23cm) and you'll have plenty of room.

2 Don't forget that the mounting frames take up a ¼ inch (6mm) all round.

3 Use visual layout sheets to make your preparation task easier.

Image density

Clear, striking visuals result from originals where image density provides the right contrast between elements of the layout. To ensure that your image density is right, follow these steps:

1 Make sure that all type and artwork is carbon based i.e. India ink, a number 2B pencil, carbon typewriter ribbon, printed material etc. And it must all be black.

2 Ensure that the original can be reproduced in a plain-paper copier. Run a plain paper copy first to check the original.

3 Use the right paper. Hard surfaced papers provide a more even imaging quality than watermark, bond or other soft papers.

4 If you do make a mistake, don't use liquid corrector, or chalk cover-ups. Instead, erase completely or cut out and replace.

Lettering systems

There is little doubt that bold, crisp, professionally prepared letters can really make your overhead transparency sparkle.

The lettering systems that are available today range from simple self-adhesive letters and numerals to sophisticated lettering machines which do the job faster. Here are a few tips on when to invest in more sophisticated lettering systems.

1 How important is the presentation? A top level financial presentation really needs to be clean, neat and professional.

2 How much time do you have to prepare all of the lettering? If time is short, you may be better off investing in a machine.

3 Will you need multiple copies of the overhead transparencies (say for distribution to other sales offices)? If you do, the originals should be perfect.

4 How much time does lettering take for the transparencies you do now? If it's a lot, think about using a machine.

You will realize that careless lettering can detract from the best visual and neat, well-planned lettering can be effective even without an illustration.
Here are some tips for ensuring that your lettering is up to standard.

1 Typewriters. Be careful when using your machine for visual copy. Most typefaces are too small or faint but special faces can be obtained which work well.

2 Hand lettering. Be neat and use large lettering. Letters should be at least ¼ inch (6mm) high and laid out evenly. Use a ruler placed across the original or a sheet of lined notebook paper underneath.

3 Stencils. A stencil is a helpful guide to uniform lettering. Trace by pushing the pen or pencil into the letter and drawing round the inside edge.

4 Tracing. Use a sharp pen or pencil. Check your art stores for textbooks on lettering.

Making your own visuals

Discover your talents

If you have the talent, design and draw your own visual originals freehand. You'll find that you don't need to be an accomplished artist to get quite pleasing results. Here are a few professional secrets for you to follow.

1 Aim for simplicity in your drawings. Too much detail will often be lost or become irrelevant when the artwork is projected.

2 Practise with some of the new magic markers in dark inks. They give good solid lines which are ideal for projection.

3 Don't be afraid to try – and try again. You'll develop your own style from your repeated efforts.

Investigate available sources

You'd be surprised at what you can find in books, magazines and papers. They are great sources of subject matter for visuals. Everyone who prepares overhead projection visuals will want to start saving interesting illustrations to build an extensive personal resources file.

1 Whenever you see a bold visual or illustration, cut it out for your file.

2 If you're thinking of a topic to visualize, check through your resources file. The right visual will click with the right text without your even thinking about it.

3 Either paste up the visual on your original artwork, or if it is too light, trace over it with a sharp black pen or pencil.

Prepared original pads

Many of the visuals that you prepare may be standard types of graph, maps or other symbols. You could save a lot of time and trouble by using 3M's prepared original pads. These basic visual originals are printed in ready-to-image black on special sheets that speed the preparation of finished originals.

Now you're ready to make a transparency

You're now ready to begin making transparencies from the original you have created. You can breathe life and colour into the black and white masters to add emphasis, clarity and impact. At this stage, it may be worth your while to remember all you have learned so far about making effective visuals.

1 Visual images must be large enough for the audience to see. Is this true for the originals you now have in hand?

2 Visualized information must be easy to understand. Are your black and white masters easy to understand?

3 The visual must highlight, reinforce and add to the commentary of the presenter. Does yours?

If the answers are all yes, move on to the next phase.

Which technique do you choose?

You're now at the stage when you have to put your carefully prepared original into the production stage to make one or more overhead transparencies per original. You're faced with a choice of how to do this. You can either use an infrared copier, or you can use the plain-paper copier in your office. Here are some advantages of the infrared process:

1 Compact. They're also light and can be moved around easily.

2 Fast. Feed your original transparency into the machine and in four seconds you have your imaged transparency.

3 Versatile. Spirit masters, stencil masters, laminations and paper copiers can all be produced on these machines.

4 Wide variety of films available.

Using your plain-paper copier

Until now, you may have thought of your copier in terms of paper copies only. Now you can make it more than that. Plain-paper copiers transparency film can be imaged directly in your plain-paper copier to produce clear transparencies for overhead projection.

Plain-paper copier film doubles the duties of a plain paper copier simply by replacing the paper, and transparencies can be used on most of the plain-paper copiers available today.

Getting good copies from your plain-paper copier

Below are some general instructions for getting good transparencies from your plain-paper copier. Specific instructions for each type of film and each plain-paper copier are included in every body of 3M plain-paper copier transparency film.

1 Create the original.

2 Run a paper copy of the original to determine image quality. Clean and adjust your machine if the copies turn out muddy or grey.

3 Place the correct type of film in the copier's tray.

4 Place your original on the clean copy table and copy as you would normally do. You now have an excellent transparency or transparencies.

Framing the transparency

An overhead projection transparency can be projected unframed but there are good reasons why you should frame it. The frame blocks out the light around the sides of the transparency. It adds rigidity for easy handling and storage and it provides a border area for writing notes on.

How to frame.

1 Lay the frame upside down on a flat surface.

2 Centre the transparency face down on the frame.

3 Tape all four corners and then the sides for a more secure visual.

The final sparkle

You can add the final sparkle to your transparency with just a little more effort. This can turn a good visual into an exceptional or sometimes brilliant one.

The amount of effort you put into producing transparencies really depends on the kind of presentation you are preparing. If you have a lot to gain from the outcome of the meeting, then the maximum effort is required. If the meeting is of low importance, just make it quick and simple.

But when you really want to get that message across with impact and sparkle, follow these guidelines:

Colour transparency film This is the simplest and easiest way to add interest and eye appeal to a presentation. Vary the four plain-paper copier colour films with clear and it will automatically command more attention. You can produce additional colours by placing a sheet of one colour over a sheet of another colour.

1 Lay your framed visual face down on the desk.
2 Overlay with colour transparency film and secure with Scotch tape.
3 Add other colour transparency films to obtain different colour effects. Each layer of film reduces the amount of light passing through the transparency. Project the transparency to make sure you have not added one overlay film too many.

Colour adhesive film Colour adhesive film comes in a range of six colours and can make your visuals more lively. After overlaying a sheet of write-on film to the visual, stick down a piece of the colour adhesive film to cover roughly the area you want highlighted.

1 Line up one edge of the colour adhesive film with one edge of the image.
2 Remove the backing slowly while adhering the adhesive film to the overlay film.
3 Cut around the image being careful to cut only the adhesive colour film.
4 Peel off the excess adhesive film and you have a truly effective visual.

Coloured pens and pencils A variety of specially made 3M pens offers another way of adding colour to transparencies which have been covered with a sheet of write-on film. Permanent and water-soluble colours are available, which are non-fading and project beautifully.

Billboarding This technique highlights a specific area on a visual. A sheet of colour film is taped to the mounting frame over the imaged original. A section is then cut out of the overlay film and removed.

1 Tape the unimaged colour film of your choice over the mounted transparency.

2 Using a sharp knife, cut around the section you wish to highlight but be careful to cut only the colour film.

Overlays This method helps simplify difficult concepts and also lets the presenter build up the story in an easy, step by step process.

It involves the use of two or more imaged transparencies overlaid in sequence during the presentation.

1 Hinge the overlay transparency to the frame on one side with Scotch tape to allow the base visual to be presented first.

2 Just flip over the hinged visual to add information to the projected message.

3 Try not to use more than two overlays per frame because each overlay transparency cuts down the amount of light passing through to the screen.

Filing and cataloguing transparencies

After the presentation is over, visuals should be catalogued for reference and filed for re-use or storage.

1 Write a 'Subject' and 'Number' reference on the 3M frames.

2 Fill in these items clearly for each visual.

3 Store away each visual sequentially using the frame boxes.

4 Identify the subject in the space provided on the outside of the box.

Remember, filing and cataloguing may not seem important but your presentation could be needed again at some time. If it's filed properly, you'll be able to retrieve it quickly and easily.

Visual aids

Blackboards

Advantages
No mechanisms to go wrong;
flexible; quickly erased;
mistakes easily corrected.

Disadvantages
Chalk is messy to use; creates
a classroom atmosphere;
difficult to erase well if old;
suitable for small groups only;
not portable.

Whiteboards

Similar advantages as
blackboard; also presentation
clearer with special pens; easy
and cleaner to use.

Limited to small groups;
generally only available in
training rooms; not portable.

Flip chart

Easy to use; not much can go
wrong; readily available;
cheap; versatile – can be used
pre-written or constructed
during the course of the talk;
portable.

Can be difficult to write on
quickly; only suitable for small
audiences of less than 35.

Overhead projectors

Transparencies easily and
economically produced by
hand or photocopiers; flexible;
possible to change order of
slides during presentation;
slides can be omitted; build up
of information possible with
several slides; information can
be revealed step by step;
screen is bright and clear in
normal room light; suitable for
small or large audiences;

Can break down or suffer bulb
failure, usually fan cooled and
produces background noise
which can be distracting; must
be constantly switched off so
as not to leave irrelevant
material or a blank screen
showing; speaker has to be
careful not to obscure
audience's view of the screen;
projector can also block the
view.

commands attention; easily available; smaller projectors are portable; can be used like the flip chart with a continuous roll of acetate so that the speaker can write calculations or notes on to it. Professional slides can be produced for more impact or continuous use.

35mm slides

Very sharp bright image; focuses attention of audience; wide variety of material can be shown; easily stored and carried; projectors readily available fast and smooth operation; suits any size audience; least expensive method of showing colour artwork; useful for more formal method of presentation.

Low light makes it difficult for audience to make notes and for the speaker to maintain eye contact; less flexible than overhead projector; cannot change order or omit slides; artwork can be expensive; assistant needed for projection unless remote control is available.

Physical objects

Can save a lot of unnecessary description; ensures everyone has uniform idea of what speaker is talking about; members of the audience can handle them – direct contact is always useful; versatile; models; objects and props often easily available.

Passing round objects is time consuming and distracting; small groups only, holding up article unsuitable for small objects or large audiences. Models can be expensive to prepare.

15 Humour and wit

Once you get people laughing they are listening and you can tell them almost anything
Herbert Gardner

I have to admit that I debated whether or not to write this chapter, because I find the subject of humour difficult. However, I suspect that you may feel the same and for that reason, I decided to include a few suggestions on how to make your audience smile. The humour I am describing isn't intended to provoke helpless laughter in your audience. If you are able to achieve this and you feel it appropriate for a business presentation, you won't need to read what I've got to say. Alternatively, you may feel uneasy about attempting to be funny and you may worry that you will run the risk of ruining a good talk by including what turns out to be an unamusing witticism. If you feel like this, remember that there is no obligation to be humorous. But, if you can do so successfully, there are several advantages.

Why include humour?

Humour at the beginning of the presentation relaxes the audience and also eases the tension for you. Audiences, even a small group, sense the apprehension you feel as you stand to speak to them and they want to be reassured that they are in good hands. By giving them something to laugh at, you show that you are in control. Smiling and laughing together unites an audience and creates an atmosphere in which they will listen together. An audience of local businessmen enjoyed this comment from a bank manager. 'It seems to me that many people look on a visit to their bank manager with the same dread as a visit to the dentist. Really we're not that bad.' You can establish a rapport with the audience by using humour so that they feel well-disposed towards you, which is particularly important if you are selling ideas or products.

Humour is useful to lighten a heavy and possibly dull passage in your talk and to make it more digestible and therefore more memorable. Take a look at your own experience, your own background and the subject area you're talking about to find stories that are funny and which prompt a small smile of recognition on people's faces. You can also use it to illustrate major points or the transition between them.

What is humour?

The humour which is suitable for a business presentation is difficult to classify, but it may be helpful to describe what it is not. Jokes are risky because they require a positive reaction from the audience and if it's not forthcoming, it is obvious that the joke has flopped. A joke that fails to raise a smile causes embarrassment for you and for the audience and has the opposite effect to the one that you intended. Professional comedians will tell you that audiences vary enormously and a joke which was successful one night, may not even raise a titter on another. Ask yourself if you can afford to misjudge what will be an acceptable joke for your audience? Even when your joke is pertinent, you may ruin its effect by incorrect timing, emphasizing the wrong word or, worse still, getting the punch line muddled up. You may be a proficient joke teller within your group of friends, but it takes a special talent to deliver a joke successfully to larger audiences. My advice is to avoid them. There are other ways of including humour in your talk which don't require such a positive and therefore obvious reaction from the audience, and which, if unsuccessful, will not cause embarrassment to you or the audience.

The safest target for your humour is yourself. Show them your weaknesses and admit your failings. Tell stories against yourself. For instance, I remember the occasion when as a guest speaker at a luncheon, I was waiting to be introduced. The Chairman turned to me and asked if I was ready to begin and unfortunately added, 'Or shall we allow them to enjoy themselves a little longer?'

You may find that some of the best humour arises out of the situation, so don't be self-conscious about voicing a comment if it springs to mind. But never use the words, 'That reminds me of a story about . . .' because the tale that follows is usually irrelevant.

If you intend using humour in your talk to make people smile, you must know how to identify shared experiences and problems. Your humour must be relevant to the audience and should help to show them that you are one of them or that you understand their situation and are in sympathy with their point of view. Depending on whom you are addressing, the problems will be different. If you are talking to a group of managers, you may refer to the disorganized methods of their secretaries, alternatively if you are addressing secretaries, you may want to comment on their disorganized bosses. A management audience will probably respond to a witty remark about coping with unions and an audience of union members will appreciate a remark criticizing management.

Here is an example, which I heard at a nurses' convention, of a story which works well because the audience all shared the same view of doctors. A man arrives in heaven and is being shown around by St Peter. He sees wonderful accommodation, beautiful gardens, sunny weather, and so on. Everyone is very peaceful, polite and friendly until, waiting in a queue for lunch, the new arrival is suddenly pushed aside by a man in a white coat, who rushes to the head of the line, grabs his food and stomps over to a table by himself. 'Who is that?' the new arrival asked St Peter. 'Oh, that's God', came the reply, 'but sometimes he thinks he's a doctor!'

If you are part of the group which you are addressing, you will be in a position to know the experiences and problems which are common to all of you and it'll be appropriate for you to make a passing remark about the inedible canteen food or the chairman's notorious bad taste in ties. With other audiences you mustn't attempt to gatecrash with humour, as they will resent an outsider making disparaging remarks about their canteen or their chairman. You will be on safer ground if you stick to scapegoats like the Post Office, the telephone system, poor service from garages and banks, as well as the vagaries of the weather.

If you feel awkward being humorous, you must practise so that it becomes more natural. Include a few casual and apparently off-the-cuff remarks which you can deliver in a relaxed and unforced manner. Often it's the delivery which causes the audience to smile, so speak slowly and remember that a raised eyebrow or a quizzical look may help to show that you are making a lighthearted remark.

Look for the humour. It often comes from the unexpected. A twist on a familiar quote, 'If at first you don't succeed, give up', 'The darkest hour is just before you're overdrawn' or a play on words or on a situation. Search for exaggeration and understatements. Look at your talk and pick out a few words or sentences which you can turn about and inject with humour.

You'll also find humour in your everyday life. Look back to yesterday and you'll remember something which may not have seemed funny at the time but which would be so in retelling.

Build a humour file

There are several books available which purport to contain humour and wit. I have listened to highly amusing speakers who have incorporated stories and anecdotes in their talks which I know to have originated from these sources but I think it takes a particularly discerning eye to recognize a funny story in print. The secret of employing what I call 'second hand humour' is to personalize it so that it appears to be your own experience. Here's an example:

A young man who was just about to embark on a business career went to see his grandfather, who had founded the family firm. 'Remember, my boy, that in business honesty is still the best policy'.

'Right, grandfather' said the grandson.

'But before you do anything else, read up on Company Law', recommended the old man. 'You would be surprised at the kinds of thing that you can do in the name of business and still be honest.'

You can modify this story by recalling the advice that your own father gave you when you started work; 'He told me that in business honesty is the best policy. He also advised me to read up on Company Law because as he put it, "You'd be surprised at the kinds of thing you can do in the name of business and still be honest".'

Reading this story you'll probably not find it particularly amusing but remember that in the right context and with the appropriate audience it will provide a light-hearted moment.

If you are talking to a group of people you know well, you can substitute the name of a mutual colleague in order to personalize the story, 'I understand that Adam Sums, our new accountant, was asked by the managing director during his interview "What is ten times ten?" Apparently he made his mark by replying, "That rather depends on the figure you had in mind sir."'

Looking through books of humour is time consuming and should only be undertaken in small chunks, as after a while nothing seems to be amusing. Try putting these books by the side of the toilet or by your bed so that you can read a few stories at a time and judge them individually.

Keep a cuttings file of news about your industry or profession. You may find that you can link several incidents into a humorous story. Steal other people's ideas and anecdotes if they help to illustrate your point of view.

Keep a file of case histories, examples and stories which you have found funny and which you'll be able to use in future. You'll only be able to use it if you keep track of it. Ideas just fly away if you don't capture them on paper in such a way that you can find them when you need them.

You can watch television programmes like 'The Two Ronnies' and crib from them. Many of their scripts are now available in book form and some of their one-liners are useful to add a sparkle to your talk. But be careful only to use material which is relevant

to the audience. Also beware of sexist stories which will antagonize women, and avoid religious and racialist comments.

If you do use material from a known comic you can preface
your remarks by using his name. For example, 'On the subject of
politicians, I agree with Ronnie Barker when he said that they
have a lot in common with chimpanzees – the higher they climb
the more unpleasant features they reveal.' Incidentally this is a
story that can be adapted to suit any audience or group of people
by substituting the appropriate word for politicians. Here is
another example, 'Bob Hope put it well when he described banks
as a place who will lend you money only if you can prove that you
don't need it.'

How to deliver a humorous line

Humour should never be announced. 'I must tell you an amusing
thing my father said to me . . .'. This kills the story. Your wit
must appear to be a spontaneous throw-away comment which
the audience can choose to smile at. If you tell them beforehand
that they will find it funny, they will be expecting an exceptionally good story. Unannounced humour makes the audience feel
that they have individually recognized the fun side of your
character. It's the difference between having a good meal in an
unknown restaurant that you have personally discovered and
having a good meal in a highly recommended restaurant. The
first meal will be unexpected and therefore, will seem better, even
if it is not. The most successful humour is the unexpected peep
behind the serious exterior. Your delivery mustn't indicate that
you are telling an amusing story. A twinkle in your eye is more
appealing than laughter and giggles at your own witticisms.
Remember to slow down for the punchline and be careful to
enunciate every word. For instance, 'An advertisement which
makes you think you've longed for something for years but have
just never heard of it.' 'He's the kind of chap who has plenty to be
modest about.' 'I just can't stand intolerance.'

Beware of relying on an accent or dialect to be amusing – you
may find it difficult to reproduce it accurately under stress.

Never read anecdotes, humorous stories or jokes, as they'll sound artificial and forced. Your humour should appear to be spontaneous and uncontrived and you can't achieve this naturalness if you are reading every word. You also need plenty of eye contact to judge how your humour is being received.

Timing is crucial if your humour is to succeed. This is a combination of pausing between words and sentences, and phrasing which is grouping words together. Record one of your favourite comedians and analyse how he/she uses pauses effectively. Try to stress the important words. For instance, 'A chap who had *plenty* to be *modest* about'. Pause after your humorous line, but quickly pick up the thread of your talk after the audience has reacted. If there is no response don't agonize, simply continue in a calm unruffled manner. Some of the audience may be smiling inside. You are not a comic and the success of your presentation doesn't depend on your ability to bring the house down. I know from experience that audiences can respond differently to the same line and if an expected smile doesn't materialize, you must carry on with the rest of your talk. I prefer to stick to one-liners because they can pass unnoticed if they don't succeed, and not throw you off course.

Inexperienced speakers will often swallow or mumble humorous remarks because they are concerned that they won't be considered funny by the audience. That's a sure-fire path to failure. Don't include humour if you feel uncomfortable about speaking out. You need courage and confidence to win a round of smiles.

Like all speaking, your humour must be researched and practised until you feel comfortable and familiar with it. Your body language and facial expressions as well as your timing are most important. Memorize your humorous lines so that you can look at your audience. Witty, light-hearted comments which are self deprecating or which knock a common enemy are more effective than long elaborate jokes. Aim to tickle the audience's mind.

Summary – humour and wit

- Humour unites audiences.
- Use common problems and shared experiences.
- Avoid telling jokes.
- Collect funny stories.
- Never read your humorous lines.
- Aim for chuckles, not for belly laughs.

16 Writing a script to be read

The difficulty of speeches is that you're perpetually poised between the cliché and the indiscretion.
Harold Macmillan

How to write spoken English

As I have been writing this book, I have been imagining you reading it – in fact, I have tried to imagine having a conversation with you. It may be one sided but I wanted to talk to you, as I find it easier to talk than to write. You will have noticed that my style is informal. But at first, I found it quite difficult to write like this, as I was inhibited by having a pen in my hand.

Unless you are a professional script writer, it's probable that whenever you write, your words will be read and not listened to. Written English is what we are trained to write and you may find it difficult to adopt a different style when you have to write spoken English. If you have ever seen the transcript of someone talking naturally, you'll have noticed that the sentences are short and sometimes even unfinished; the vocabulary may appear repetitious while other words may be rarely used. You'll also see that many of the sentences are ungrammatical although the speaker may be well educated. If you write a script that is grammatically correct, it may sound rather formal. Here is an everyday example of written and spoken English illustrating this point. In answer to 'who is it?' how many people say 'it is I'? Most will say 'it's me'. It may be grammatically correct to say 'for whom is that telephone call?' but most people will say 'who's that phone call for?'

Use a simple vocabulary

It's not only grammar which changes when we write to speak, it's also the choice of words and the style of sentence. Undoubtedly, your written vocabulary is larger than your spoken vocabulary. However, if you employ words which are not in everyday use, although they may look right on the paper, they will sound artificial when spoken. Remember, you are not seeking to impress your audience with your academic knowledge – your objective should be to explain your ideas clearly and precisely, so that your audience understands immediately. Of course, if you normally use an extensive vocabulary in your everyday speech and you're sure that your audience will understand, you shouldn't feel inhibited in using it. If you have difficulty in pronouncing a word, don't use it because under stress you'll stumble and appear uncomfortable.

Here is an example of written vocabulary and spoken vocabulary. 'Successful script writers ensure that they utilize a vocabulary which is comprehensible to a specific audience'. Translated into spoken English, this becomes 'Make sure you only use words your audience understands'.

Short, simple sentences are best

Sentence structure can cause problems for novice scriptwriters as they tend to use too many conjunctions and not enough full stops. A useful exercise when you have finished writing your script is to go through it and cross out all conjunctions, i.e., and so, however, but, nevertheless, etc. and replace them with full stops. It may *look* wrong, but it will *sound* right. The best test of your script is to read it aloud. How does it sound? Would you really express yourself that way? Is it wordy and contrived? It should be natural and simple.

Always ensure that the main point comes at the beginning of your sentence, followed by any qualifying phrases. This is the exact reverse of correct written English. Here is an example of correct written English: 'Provided that our new warehouse is open in July and our sales figures for domestic appliances continue to show an upward trend in Germany, I am going to recommend that we expand our export drive to France'. Here is the same sentence translated into spoken English: 'I am going to recommend we expand our export drive to France, provided that our new warehouse is open in July and our sales figures for domestic appliances continue to show an upward trend in Germany.' This sequence of ideas is important because as listeners we cannot hold qualifying phrases in suspension, waiting to hear the total sentence before we can understand the point. You may know the end of your sentence, but your listeners won't.

More pitfalls to avoid

When we compose written English, we often employ the passive voice, e.g. 'hand movements are to be controlled by speakers when addressing an audience.' If you employ this voice in your script, it will sound academic and remote. Instead, use an active voice, e.g. 'You should control your hand movements when you're addressing an audience.'

Remember that when we speak, we abbreviate words. Cannot becomes can't, would not becomes wouldn't. Make sure your script does not have any unabbreviated words or you will read them and it will sound artificial.

Have you heard speakers refer to the 'point above'? In spoken English this should be 'my last point' or 'the point I've just made'.

How to type a script

Here are some suggestions on the layout of your script which will make it easier to read. Remember that the lighting at the lectern may not be very bright and therefore your script must be clear and simple to read.

- Use a word processor if possible so that changes can be made quickly and painlessly.
- Use a large typeface or have your script enlarged on a photocopier, and use both upper and lower case.
- Use double or triple spaces between lines and twice that between paragraphs.

- Use wide margins.
- Only type on one side of the paper.
- Spell out numbers in words, e.g. three thousand four hundred and fifty pounds and not £3450.
- Don't continue a sentence from one page to another.
- Number each page.
- Don't staple pages together.
- Mark visual aids in the margin in colour.

Summary: How to write a script that sounds natural

- Read the chapter on Writing a Script.
- Don't worry excessively about the grammar.
- Use simple but precise words.
- Keep your sentences short.
- Abbreviate words like cannot, do not, etc.
- Read it aloud several times to test its naturalness.

17 Hints on reading a script

In a previous chapter I described the disadvantages of reading a script, but there may be occasions when you can't avoid it. You may want to ensure that no essential points are omitted which could lead to misunderstanding, particularly if you are likely to be quoted by the press or when your words may be legally binding; you could be presenting a particularly sensitive policy statement or you may be making a speech for a political party.

Reading a paper

For some reason there is a tradition that scientific or technical papers are read. I find this discourteous to the audience as they have come to hear a talk and not a 'reading'. If you are presenting a paper at a conference or convention, you may also have to submit your speech in advance so that it can be given to the delegates in the conference folder. If this is the case, consider how you can enliven your presentation with additional new material – do you have any anecdotes or personal stories which might illustrate the main points of your talk? These might be unsuitable for inclusion in the paper which is distributed to the conference delegates, but they would add to the audience's enjoyment of your talk. Explain some of the problems you have encountered and any doubts that you may have had about resolving them. In this way, the audience is gaining from having come to listen to you; if you simply read a script to them, they might feel that they could have stayed at home and read it for themselves. Pay them the compliment of disclosing more of yourself than you might want to put into the paper.

Complex audio-visual productions

You will need to have a written script if you are reading your talk on autocue. If you are involved in an elaborate production with slide presentations and video, you will be expected to give voice cues to the projectionist. He will be following your script and as you reach certain words, he will activate the appropriate visual. It is possible to work without a script on this kind of production, but it can lead to mistakes such as the wrong visual appearing or visuals getting out of synchronization, which looks unprofessional and loses credibility for the speaker.

Using a teleprompter

A few years ago only TV presenters used teleprompters – often also called Autocue (which is, in fact, a brand name). Then it was discovered by politicians and now it's not uncommon to find it in front of business speakers throughout the country.

It consists of a one-way mirror (screen) which is placed in front of you and on to which your script is projected. The audience can see your face through the screen and as you read the words on the screen, you appear to be looking through it at the audience. Your talk is prepared on a typewriter or word processor and printed on to a roll of paper or computer stationery and relayed by closed circuit TV cameras through monitors near to the speaking point. From the monitor it's reflected on to the one way mirror or screen in front of you. The operator, hidden from the audience, carefully follows the speed at which you are speaking and moves the roll of script.

Advantages of using a teleprompter

Using a teleprompter means that you can read your entire script and also maintain eye contact with the audience. With several display screens in appropriate positions, you can walk about and appear to be talking naturally with no notes or prompts. Even sophisticated audiences who recognize the display screens, will glass

lectern

stand

monitor

master unit

The distance between the master and presenter units is unlimited

How a teleprompter works

quickly forget that they are being used once the speaker starts to talk.

If you use spectacles to read, you may find that you don't need them to read a teleprompter as the print is very large with only four words to the line. This is particularly helpful if you normally have the problem of having to take your spectacles off in order to look at the audience or to look at your notes.

A smaller table top unit, for informal boardroom meetings, which can be operated by the speaker, can also be useful.

How to use a teleprompter like a pro

- Make sure your script is sent to the teleprompt company with sufficient time to make last minute changes. Although word processors are used universally and changes can be made effortlessly, when several speakers want to modify and amend their talks at the eleventh hour, there could be problems for the audio visual production team. Remember that they operate from voice cues, so if you change your script you must re-position the cues to indicate when your visuals should be projected. Send your script approximately five to seven days before the date of your presentation so that it can be typed out for the teleprompt camera.
- Don't add too many instructions to yourself, e.g. 'MD crosses over to left of stage. I introduce sales manager'. TV scripts are full of stage instructions and the professional overlooks them, but you will only find them confusing if you see them on the screen. The teleprompt display screen is approximately 12" × 8" and shows six to seven lines, so if you fill the screen with instructions, you will need to pause for a few moments before you continue speaking.
- Ask for a copy of your script typed on the teleprompt roll so that you can practise reading it aloud. It's useful to become familiar with the four words per line format.
- Allow at least two full run-throughs with the teleprompt company at the venue of your conference or meeting. Often you will find that coaching in the use of this type of

teleprompter is included in the hire charge. You should take
advantage of this.

■ The height of the screen can be adjusted for different
speakers; however, if the screen is placed vertically, this
allows for a greater range of speakers' heights without the
need for adjustment.

■ If possible, use two screens at each lectern as this gives you
the flexibility to move your head more naturally from side to
side.

Some don'ts

■ Don't stare at the screen – look away from time to time.
■ Don't speak too quickly – the operator will move the script
according to the speed of your delivery.
■ Don't clutch the lectern – make appropriate hand gestures.
■ Don't keep your head in a rigid position – relax and move it
naturally.
■ Don't frown – look pleasant and remember to smile!

Final warning

If you have a good, natural script and you learn to use the
teleprompter well, it can help you to be a better speaker, but you
must allow sufficient time to become familiar with the technique.
You have to learn to *read well*; not everyone can do this and you
may find that you feel more confident using another form of
delivery.

How to make your script sound natural

I have suggested techniques you can follow to write a script in
spoken English and not written English in the previous chapter,
but words alone will not convince your audience. Most of your
impact must come from your voice and your visual appearance.
Reading a script limits your body language so you must rely on
your voice to express **enthusiasm** and **vitality**. Few people are
naturally good readers but it is a skill you can learn through
practice.

Reading aloud

If you are fortunate enough to have small children use them as an excuse to read aloud; they are an uncritical audience and will enjoy hearing the full range of your voice. This is an opportunity for you to experiment with exaggeration – loud and soft – fast and slow – high and low. Use the full repertoire of your vocal range.

If you have no children you can still read aloud from the newspaper, from a book or from a play. Learn to read ahead a few words, look up at an imaginary audience and deliver those words. With practice you will feel less dependent on the text. The more eye contact you can make with the audience, the more they will listen.

Practise, practise, practise

Once you have the typed copy of your script, read it aloud straight through. You will find that there are many words which sound awkward and sentences which feel clumsy. Amend them so that they sound and feel comfortable for you. If you have the misfortune to have to read a script prepared by someone else you will need to allow extra time to personalize it. Don't feel that the scriptwriter is the expert and his words are cast in stone. I have seen too many speakers stumbling their way through unfamiliar words and sentence constructions, embarrassing both the audience and themselves in the process. You must be the judge of what sounds natural for you. So modify, cut and add until you feel at ease with the script. But do put a time limit on the changes or you'll only have a final draft minutes before you are due to speak!

I was recently called to train a senior manager two days before an annual conference at which she was due to speak and although the script had been prepared for her, she had failed to find time to read it before our first training session. We spent several hours together, as I insisted she read and re-read the entire talk out loud. Eventually she was able to inject some colour into her voice as well make some eye contact with the audience.

You don't need a speech consultant to sit with you. Save yourself money and use your own self-discipline to rehearse several times. But silent readings don't count, it must be out loud.

Try these techniques

Practise reading ahead and raising your eyes as you say the last few words of each sentence. Look down, read the first few words of the next sentence, look up, and deliver them to your audience.

- Don't gabble because you have the full text in front of you – remember how effective pauses can be.
- Use your full voice repertoire – vary the speed and the pitch, use loud and soft for emphasis.
- Try to keep your head up so that your voice carries.
- Use facial expression to add impact to your talk.
- Don't turn over each page as you finish the last line, simply slide it across.
- If you need spectacles don't keep removing them during your speech. Use half glasses and look over the top of them, simply letting your eyes come up and sweep over the rows of faces.
- Remember to arrange for a lectern on which you can rest your speech.
- Practise with a tape recorder or a video camera until you sound and look as if you are talking naturally.

Establishing contact before you begin to read

Reading a script may make you seem impersonal and remote but you can reduce this effect by establishing contact with your audience before you begin reading. Start with a personal story which you can deliver without referring to your script or involve the audience by asking them a question.

I began a talk on controlling nerves once by walking to the front of the stage and asking how many people would feel nervous in my position. Up shot the hands. Then I asked one or two of them to describe how they felt when they were nervous. Then I involved other people in the audience by asking whether they shared these symptoms. This short involving technique immediately raised the audience's interest level. Use a similar technique before you begin to read a script, and you will reveal more of yourself than you can when you are hidden behind a lectern.

Reading is a poor method of communicating your thoughts, but at least if you have a good script and can deliver it well, you have a better chance of keeping your listeners' attention. Finally, do remember what one wit said: 'reading a script is like courting through a fence – you can hear every word but there's not a lot of contact'.

Summary: how to read with impact

- Practise reading aloud from newspapers or from a book.
- Rehearse your talk aloud until it is very familiar.
- Learn to read ahead and look up at the audience.

18 Persuading, convincing and selling

Everyone lives by selling something.
Robert Louis Stevenson

There are some people who think selling is a dirty word. For them, the very idea of a salesman conjures up a picture of a pushy, fast-talking individual whose sole aim is to force his customers to buy against their will. Worst of all, he doesn't listen. Faced with such a hard sale, his customers may feel that their only option is to sign on the dotted line. Most of us have experienced such horrors at one time or another and they tend to colour our view of selling.

In this chapter I want to suggest some ways in which you can improve *your* selling techniques, because, whether you recognize it or not you're involved in selling every day of your life. You may wonder how I can make such a claim. Think back over the last few days to the decisions you have made in your working environment. Were all your ideas and views totally supported by everyone who was involved? I doubt it. I imagine that you had to coax, influence, cajole, urge, even insist and impel people to follow what you believed to be the right course of action. In that process you were selling your ideas and your opinions. I have linked persuading, convincing and selling together in one chapter heading because I believe they are all part of the same skill.

One reason why you may dislike the idea of selling is because, like telling a joke, it requires a positive reaction from the listener and if the response is not forthcoming, you feel you are being rejected. This is in fact a misconception. It is your opinion or idea which is being rejected, not you. This is a hard lesson to learn. In my early days of selling, I often felt discouraged by a seemingly endless wall of 'No thank you, dear, not today'. Fortunately I was able to improve my techniques so eventually I received more acceptances than rejections. In the commercial world the reason for your speaking will often be to persuade, convince and sell. I want to draw together some of the themes which run through this book and show how you can use them to achieve support and agreement for your views more easily.

Prepare to persuade

Your first step to successful persuasion is researching your listeners. What are their concerns and what are their problems? What do you know about them? It is impossible to persuade if you don't know their present position. In an extreme case you might find that they already agree with you and need no convincing. Your listeners have views and opinions as well as difficulties and anxieties which will influence their acceptance or rejection of your ideas.

In the chapter covering Meeting the Media, I refer to open questions which managers employ to gain full and comprehensive answers. Open questions generally start with who, what, when, why, where or how. Use them to discover more about your listeners' opinions. 'What do you think the effect will be if we agree to the overtime ban?' 'How can we achieve these results in less time?' Reverse roles with your listener and let him state his case as fully as possible, but remember also to ask for reasons why he supports a particular view. If you are managing a sales force, you may need to persuade your reps of the importance of completing paperwork. If you can discover their reason for disliking it, you will be half-way to overcoming their prejudice. Sometimes people are reluctant to express their doubts or fears about a course of action, because they feel that it will reflect on their ability to complete a task. I am often faced with managers who dislike admitting that they feel nervous when speaking in public. I have to persuade them that recognizing their anxiety is the first step to controlling it.

You may be attempting to convince a colleague to change his

mind, but until you can uncover the reasons for his views, you won't be successful. His views may be based on faulty information. 'All the typists arrive late in the morning and leave early at the end of the day.' He may have had previous experience, which he has misinterpreted or which has jaundiced his thinking. If you don't identify his viewpoint and the reasons for it, your sound and well-reasoned arguments will go sailing straight past him, because they are not correctly targeted. You must have the bull's-eye in your sights before you can hit it.

Developing your listening skills

You may need to improve your listening skills before you can persuade successfully. In the first chapter, I gave reasons why listening isn't easy and I suggested some ways in which speakers could help to minimize the difficulties.

You can also help yourself to be a better listener. Remember that some of the major barriers to effective listening are internal. When, as a listener, you go down Route 350, you are allowing yourself to be distracted by your own thoughts. So concentrate and don't allow your own experience and prejudices to block out what you're hearing. Listen with an open mind to the content and disregard the distractions of irritating mannerisms and poor delivery. Personally I find this a great challenge. Much of my working day is spent assessing and correcting speakers, so that it has become second nature. When I am 'off duty' and in a social situation, I have to silence my inner thoughts such as 'what a pity she doesn't open her mouth more when she speaks' or 'why does he keep saying yes at the end of every sentence'. Don't fall into the trap of letting poor presentation prevent you from listening well.

Instead of going down Route 350, you can use your spare brain capacity to summarize mentally and to recap on what the speaker is telling you. This can be particularly useful if she is presenting information in a jumbled and unstructured manner. As each idea is presented, you can mentally categorize it so that you'll be able to recall it at a later stage.

Don't forget your body language when you are listening. Your eye contact and facial expression should be encouraging. Show your interest by smiling, nodding, saying 'I see, I understand' and asking questions, 'So why was that?'

Successful persuasion often depends upon your demonstrating an understanding of the listeners' viewpoint. Showing that you recognize their problem can help to build a rapport which increases your credibility. Don't be too quick to present your own ideas. Register that you have heard what they've told you by repeating their views. This is an indication that you have listened, not that you agree with them; e.g. 'So you're worried that if we extend the period of payment, we would have a cash flow problem?' 'So from your point of view, asking the typists to work overtime could lead to resentment?' 'I see, so you're telling me that if you installed new equipment it could cause a disruption at a very busy time of year?'

What are the needs of your listeners?

Earlier in the book in the chapter on Preparation and Planning, I mentioned satisfying some of the needs of management as well as those of the work force. Everyone has their own particular need which they seek to satisfy as well as problems which they want to solve. So find out what your listeners want. Do they have a difficulty which needs resolving? What are they hoping to achieve? What are they aiming for? It may be as simple as an afternoon in which the telephone doesn't ring or as ambitious as doubling the previous year's profits.

I remember a management consultant telling me that when she talked to a new client, she always tried to identify 'the pain'. In other words, what was causing her client anxiety. Her client might identify 'the pain' like this: 'If only we could find staff who took an interest in their jobs . . .' or 'If only we could be sure of getting the spare parts on time . . .' Find out what is your listeners' 'if only'. What is their fantasy? Ask questions and listen to the answers.

Don't interrupt

With inarticulate long-winded speakers, it is very tempting to supply words that they are searching for or even to finish their sentences for them. Resist the temptation. It will be seen as an interruption. Don't jump in immediately the speaker has finished speaking, but allow a few seconds' silence. He will know from this that you have been listening and not simply waiting for your turn to speak. Most importantly, he will be ready to listen to you. He will feel that he doesn't have to battle with you for a chance to be heard. Therefore, your chances of persuading him are increased.

What do they know and what do they think of you?

Now that you know your listeners' position, you need to discover how much they already know about your views. You may recall from the chapter on Preparation and Planning that this level of knowledge can be multilayered:

■ What do they know?
■ What do they think they know?
■ What do they want to know?
■ What do they need to know in order for you to convince and persuade them?

If your listeners have no background information and you intend to persuade them on a new course of action, you'll need to lay some foundation before you start. On the other hand, you'll quickly lose their attention if they feel that you are talking down to them. You shouldn't underestimate the risks of miscalculating your listeners' level of understanding and knowledge.

Don't bore your colleagues in a meeting with historical facts which everyone knows. Don't do the reverse and assume that they already have sufficient information to understand your presentation. I remember vividly presenting a complex training programme to a board of directors, having already sent a written proposal to the training director. It was only later that I realized that the rest of the board had not seen the written proposal and therefore were unable to follow or understand most of my presentation.

You will also need to know what their attitude is towards you and your views. Are they:

- in favour?
- indifferent?
- opposed?

A listener who is well informed but who is opposed to you will require a different approach from one who is indifferent and uninformed.

More questions and more listening will supply the answers to help you plan your strategy for successful persuasion. To convince people, you need to appeal to their minds and to their emotions – one supports the other.

Information for their minds

Early on in your persuasion, establish why they should listen to you. Tell them what's in it for them. For example, 'I am going to show you various techniques which you can use to overcome the backlog in the warehouse'. Remember, you shouldn't tell them that you are going to convince or persuade them that one or other of the techniques is superior. This is, of course, what you may hope to do during your presentation, but it must appear that the decision is left to your listeners.

Expand on what they already know and add new points. If their level of knowledge is minimal, you may decide to present your information in a series of talks, rather than at one session. There is a limit to the amount of new material which can be absorbed at any one time. As you present the reasons for your opinions, remember to identify the areas of mutual agreement. 'You will see that we both agree on . . .' In this manner you will demonstrate your acceptance of some of your listeners' views which will provide a favourable climate in which to discuss the more controversial points. Try to minimize your differences and discount your minor points of disagreement; so that you can concentrate on persuading them to accept your views on the larger issues.

You will recall from the chapter on Writing a Talk that you need to summarize constantly and to recap. Make sure that your persuasive talk also has an easy-to-follow structure and that your ideas are illustrated with relevant examples.

Appeal to the emotions

Facts and information on their own won't change anyone's mind. You must show why your ideas will benefit the listeners. This is where your probing questions at the beginning of your meeting pay off. You know what sort of people you are facing. You have assessed what makes them tick. Simply convert your facts into advantages for them. Demonstrate how your solution can solve their problem. Explain how you can cater for their needs. Be sure to describe advantages which are relevant to *them*.

Here are a few examples of facts followed by advantages:

This is a book on effective speaking (fact). Reading it will help you to present your ideas in a convincing manner (advantage).

It is a short book (fact). Therefore it's easy to carry and you can read it anywhere (advantage).

It is reasonably priced (fact). You can become a more effective speaker than your colleagues for a small outlay (advantage).

Another interesting example of facts and advantages or features and benefits was described to me by a fellow trainer. She said 'You don't sell the drill, you sell the holes'. No one buys a drill because it has the most impressive features, you buy a drill because of its ability to make holes.

In order to convert facts or information into an advantage for your listeners, you must ask yourself what will this do for them? What benefit will this provide? What need will this satisfy? Your listeners will not buy ideas unless they recognize that they have a problem which your ideas will solve. But once having seen the need, they will be more receptive to the advantages and benefits of your ideas, provided they satisfy that need. In fact they may be uninterested in the facts and only interested in the advantages that they provide. You may choose to begin by showing the benefits which appeal to their emotions and follow them with a logical description of the facts. Changes of attitude and decision making can depend as much on an emotional response as on rational arguments.

Make it easy for them to agree

Don't expect to convert your listeners to your views instantly. No one likes to admit that they are wrong so make it easy for them. Encourage them to contribute by allowing them to acknowledge some of the benefits. Persuasion is often achieved by letting the listeners talk themselves into accepting your point of view. Sometimes you can smooth the path for them by revealing that you used to share their point of view. You can tell how a particular advantage convinced you to change your mind. In this way they keep their self-esteem while agreeing with you. Your aim is to persuade your listeners to adopt your ideas, without causing them to feel that they are 'wrong' and that you are 'right'.

With practice, you will be able to convince listeners that your solution was really theirs. Counsellors learn the art of non-judgemental listening until their clients work out their own problems. You may need to push and prod your listener towards your selected goal but it's surprising how often people will adopt new ideas with little resistance providing they feel that they haven't been forced into it. So steer clear of the hard sell.

Ask for commitment

Make sure that your listeners are committed to your ideas and if necessary, that an agreement is reached on the action which should follow, i.e. 'So we are agreed that we'll keep the front office open between Christmas and the New Year but the factory will be closed during that period. How shall we announce this decision?' Once a commitment has been made, steer clear of any further discussion and refrain from looking triumphant.

A convincing delivery

To convince and persuade successfully you must have personal commitment. You must believe in your cause and be able to show that you do. A nonchalant, unemotional presentation will fail. You must be able to show enthusiasm. It's not enough to feel it, you must display your heart on your face and in your voice. You can't read a script and hope to express heartfelt emotion. Your emotions should be, or at least appear to be, part of you. Reading a script under these circumstances indicates that you are not being honest. You need eye contact to demonstrate sincerity. Remember that the impact of your words will be diminished by poor body language. In fact if your words say one thing and your body another, you run the risk of appearing hypocritical and deceitful.

Don't allow yourself to be interrupted or distracted by comments from other members of the group. Don't allow your voice to drop at the end of each sentence. Make sure you have sufficient breath in your lungs to carry your voice to the end.

Try to match your body language to theirs. Students of body language have discovered that people who feel at ease with one another tend, unconsciously, to sit or stand in a similar fashion and to change their position to match each other. You can observe this in restaurants or in public lounges or even at office meetings. Those who are in agreement will be sitting in a similar manner. The dissenter will be leaning back or forwards to demonstrate his disagreement physically. We naturally follow this 'mirroring' of those with whom we feel comfortable, without even being aware of it. To create a harmonious atmosphere for your persuasion, try to ensure that your body language doesn't conflict with that of your listeners. Sitting back with your hands behind your head and your feet on the table while your listeners are leaning forward with their hands on the table doesn't indicate that you are trying to persuade them! I have described an extreme picture but it's surprising that people can be unaware of the impression they create with inappropriate body language. If your listener is sitting and you are standing as you try to convince him that he should work over the weekend, your chances of success will be improved if you place yourself at his level. All your communication should be face to face. The Legal Aid logo shows the outline of two people sitting, slightly inclined towards one another. It indicates an equal pair, listening and talking together. You are not seeking to intimidate or force your listeners to accept your views, so aim to balance your body language with theirs.

The adage that 'People buy people first', holds true. Often your listeners will not be assessing the value of your ideas. They will be judging *you*. If they like you, they'll want to believe in you and your opinions, even when they can find no logical reason for doing so. Appealing to people's emotions makes a lot of sense provided that this doesn't result in them feeling manipulated.

Involving techniques

However passionate a speaker you are, if you talk at your listeners continuously you won't convince or persuade them. They are likely to escape down Route 350. Remember they may want to make a point, ask a question or even to agree with you! You may want to re-read the 'Involving Techniques' section in the chapter on Audiences. Schedule pauses into your presentation so that you can invite them to contribute. 'Can you see how this new schedule would ease your workload?' or 'How do you feel this could fit into your existing budget?' or 'How does this sound to you?'

Vary the words you use to appeal to their senses. Some people can '*feel* an idea' while others want to '*hear* how it sounds' or '*see* how it's going to work'. You can identify from their conversation which category of words is most comfortable for them.

Persuasion at meetings

Various estimates have been made about the total number of hours which managers spend in meetings every year and assessments have also been made on the total cost of these meetings. In your next idle moment, maybe at an unproductive meeting, look around the room and calculate how much it is costing the company, in salaries alone, to have those people sitting at the table. The real cost is probably two or three times that sum. You can see how the company benefits and the managers save time by reducing the amount of time spent at inefficient meetings.

How to chair a meeting

Many of the skills which you will need for chairing a meeting or leading a discussion are already referred to in earlier chapters. Your planning and preparation for a meeting should fall under the same three headings:

- Setting an objective.
- Researching your audience.
- Designing a structure.

Setting an objective

Many meetings are held for the wrong reasons. Groups may follow traditional patterns of behaviour – 'We always have a meeting on Thursday afternoon' and it is often necessary to question the real purpose. Some of the more common reasons are:

- Selling ideas and products.
- Solving problems.
- Giving and getting information.
- Taking decisions.

If you are responsible for the meeting you must be clear why the meeting is taking place and what you hope it will achieve.

Make sure that a memo or a couple of phone calls couldn't accomplish as much but in less time.

Researching your audience

The many questions which you asked in preparation for being persuasive are relevant here. You should try and limit the number of people attending the meeting. An ideal number is between 6 and 7. Meetings where more than 10 are present either include silent observers or, if everyone contributes, become unmanageable. Divide up larger groups so that your meeting is more productive. Make sure that everyone is aware of the purpose of the meeting and of their own role in it. Don't invite anyone to the meeting who is not essential for achieving your objective. 'Assistants' who accompany their bosses are usually superfluous. You probably need the assistant or the boss but not both.

Designing a structure

Your preparation must include a detailed agenda which is circulated well in advanced of the meeting so that everyone has a chance to prepare. Decide whether to schedule items in order of importance or of length. Beware of short unimportant items, like deciding the new position of the notice board, which can develop into a half-hour discussion. You can often assess the likely time needed for a particular item by talking to the people concerned. If they appear to be in total disagreement you may decide to have a pre-meeting to sort out some of their differences. This will make more efficient use of the time scheduled for the main meeting.

The structure of a problem-solving meeting could be designed like this:

- Describe the problem
- Discuss the background and reasons for it
- Brainstorm solutions
- Evaluate solutions
- Give recommendations

You should aim to focus on finding solutions rather than on attributing blame.

By concentrating on finding answers, the meeting will have a more positive attitude and be more active.

Opening statements

As chairperson, your introduction sets the scene for the meeting and should stimulate interest in all the items scheduled for discussion. Try to inject a sense of urgency into the meeting so that everyone contributes. Be sure to announce the reason for the meeting and what you hope to accomplish. Also include some benefits for the participants, e.g. 'I want to finalize the budget for next year at this meeting. That means you will be able to plan your staffing requirements immediately and begin the year with a full production team.' Ensure that the time scale is understood, so that long, open-ended discussions are avoided.

Introduction

Give the background to the first item and open the discussion with a directed question, e.g. 'George, you're the one at the sharp end facing customers, can you tell us what caused this latest crisis?' You could also use an overhead question, e.g. 'So that's the situation at present. How do the rest of you think we should tackle it?'

How to control the meeting

The most powerful method of keeping control of your group is by:

- Asking questions.
- Recapping and summarizing.

I have given examples of two styles of questions in the section above and you can also use the following:

Re-directed questions   You ask another member of the group to answer a question which has been directed to you, e.g. George has stated that he will need more envelopes to complete the mailing and asks if you have any in stock. You reply 'Mary I think this is one for you. Have we received the new shipment of envelopes?'

Relay question You relay the question back to the group 'Before I answer that let me ask *you*. Where do you think we should have the Christmas party?'

Reverse question You encourage the questioner to answer his or her own question, e.g. 'What do you think? Are people prepared to pay an extra £2 for a faster service?'

Regular summaries will help people concentrate on the main points and avoid interesting but irrelevant side issues. You will remember that in your talk you included interest prompts and rhetorical questions to gather up the stragglers who had wandered off down Route 350. Summarizing during a meeting serves a similar purpose. There are two types:

■ Interim summaries.
■ Final summary.

Interim summaries You can report progress in the course of the discussion and help to refocus everyone's attention, e.g. 'Maybe we could leave the question of what happened at last year's Christmas party and try to decide where we want to have it this year. So far we've considered the Manor House which is reasonably priced but difficult to get to and the new place in the High Street which is central but we don't know if it's any good'.

With an interim summary you can also tie up one point and move on to the next, e.g. 'So we are agreed that there has been an increase in absenteeism in all the departments. The next step we need to consider is what we can do about it?'

Use interim summaries to highlight important points, e.g. 'We've covered the cost of the re-location, and the loss of production while the factory is closed. We have also looked at the disruptive factor for our staff. Those are the main points so far.'

Don't forget the value of visually displaying the main conclusion of the meeting. Use a flip chart to write up each point as it is covered. This is visual proof that you are achieving your objectives and an encouragement to the group when the discussion appears to have become bogged down.

An important effect of summarizing regularly is that it enables the minute-taker to check whether or not he/she has recorded the principal elements.

Final summary   Your final summing up should give a sense of achievement to the group. When a discussion has been heated, it's particularly important to draw together the various factions and unite them in a common course of action. As well as agreement from everyone, you need to establish commitment. Make sure that everyone present knows what they are responsible for and the time scale in which it must be accomplished.

Summary of persuading, convincing and selling

- Understand your listeners' needs.
- Appeal to their hearts as well as their minds.
- Show enthusiasm.
- Involve your listeners.
- Control the discussion.
- Get commitment.

19 Meeting the media

Beat your gong and sell your candies.
Chinese Proverb

Many of the skills which you have learnt in order to speak more effectively within your working environment also apply to press interviews, and in this chapter I am going to show how you can benefit from any interaction with the media.

At first sight you may feel that this isn't relevant to you, as you'll never have to appear on radio or TV or even be interviewed by a newspaper journalist, but consider the value of personal publicity as well as the publicity for your company and its products which is offered by any media exposure. It is free advertising. 'The business that believes that advertising is not necessary, may find that customers take the same attitude about their business.' (Anon) In fact press coverage is better than advertising. Anyone looking at an advertisement knows that it is designed and paid for by the manufacturer of the product and therefore can only present a very subjective view. Your name in print or your face on TV has much more impact as you haven't bought the space. Presenting a positive image of your company in a media interview is invaluable and consequently public relations companies spend much time attempting to obtain exposure in the press for their clients and their products.

Your immediate reaction to a press approach may be to say 'no comment' or to refer the enquirier to your company's public relations department. You may not trust the press because they seem to manipulate the truth and fail to represent accurately the views of those to whom they speak. This is a universally held view; in a recent poll journalists were rated low in integrity and honesty – in fact at about the same level as politicians! Although this is a common view of the press, it is also incorrect as far as quality papers and the broadcasting media are concerned, and for you to benefit from media contact, you must understand how the media work.

What's the angle?

Every story must have what is known as an 'angle'. This is the news hook or reason for its existence. When I was a radio journalist I often presented ideas for interviews or programmes to my producer who would immediately ask me 'why? Why is this a good story? What is the point of doing it? Who is interested?' Or more succinctly he might say, 'so what? Who cares?' These are the questions which you must ask yourself, whether you are initiating a contact with the press or responding to an approach from them. A dull rather humdrum subject can be of interest to the press provided you can identify a good angle. When I was seeking personal publicity a few years ago, I contacted a number of magazines prior to a business trip to Japan and told them that as a business woman in Japan, I was interested to discover whether I would be offered the male equivalent of a geisha girl. When I returned, I was interviewed by three different journalists on the problems and delights of travelling as a Western business woman in Japan. (No, there aren't any male equivalents to geisha girls.)

The journalists' staple diet is 'News' and yet is an undefinable term. Ask ten press men to describe what constitutes 'News' and you will receive as many different answers. However, for the purposes of this book, I will exclude the possibility of your having to be interviewed on a major news item such as an air crash, a murder or your adulterous affair with a Hollywood star.

Coping with an approach from the press

You may well be flattered as well as a little apprehensive when you find a journalist wants to talk to you and so here are some guide-lines to help you cope.

Saying no

You can refuse to speak to the press, but be sure you understand the consequences if you choose that course of action. The journalist's first contact will be by phone and when he has described why he has approached you, ask for time to think about his proposal but do return his phone call promptly as he will have deadlines to meet. On some occasions, if you decide not to meet the press, you can suggest an alternative person to represent your company or association. However, if your views are personal and you decline to be interviewed, you can offer to be quoted 'off the record'. This will enable the journalist to include your comments and maintain a balance in his story. For example, on the radio you will hear a reporter saying, 'I have spoken to several managers within the industry and the consensus is that the strike will be over by the end of the week.' Or 'sources close to the strike action committee claim that the latest pay offer will be turned down.' TV is mostly visual and 'unattributable sources', i.e. when the interviewer doesn't name his source, are quoted less frequently. On balance I advise my clients to co-operate with the press whenever possible because your 'no comment' can easily be turned into 'He refused to speak to the press' with the implication that you have something to hide.

If you have a good excuse for not wanting to speak to the press, i.e. you don't have all the facts, or you are waiting for a report, tell the journalist your reason. Always refuse to comment on statements or quotations from articles by a third party until you have seen the full text. New technology has made it possible to transmit data rapidly across the country and so you can justifiably insist that you must read the entire quote in context before responding.

Before you say yes

When you find you have a journalist on the telephone, don't be rushed into agreeing to take part in a programme or to be interviewed until you have a clear idea of what the angle is. In other words, why is the subject being covered? What makes it newsworthy? Why do they want you to contribute? Take control of the situation and of your tongue and reverse roles with the caller. Now is the time for you to interview the journalist and write down everything he says in answer to your questions. His willingness or reluctance at this stage to discuss openly the reason for and the content of his article or programme is a good indicator of his integrity. If necessary, ask him to slow down or repeat information until you are satisfied that you have enough data on which to base your decision to accept or decline his invitation. Find out his name, the name of his paper, or station and programme and when and where the interview will take place, (if you are going to be on a business trip in Australia on the day in question, you don't need to continue your conversation).

Here is a check-list of questions to ask before you agree to be interviewed:

- Why is the article being written or the programme being made?
- Why is the subject newsworthy?
- What is the angle?
- Why have you been approached?
- Who else's views are being sought?
- Who else will appear on the programme?
- Will it be broadcast live or will it be recorded?

If you are agreeable in principle, say so to the journalist at this point and tell him you will confirm later in the day or week. This allows you time to ponder on the most important question – what's in it for you? By gaining time, you may be able to watch or listen to the programme, or read the newspaper or journal if it is not familiar to you. You will also have the opportunity to seek the views of people within your company as to whether you should agree to be interviewed and to decide how the company would benefit. Here is a check list of questions for you to answer before you say yes:

- What's in it for me?
- What's in it for my company?
- Am I the best person to be interviewed?
- Do I want to be seen to associate with the other speakers?
- Do I have sufficient time to prepare?

- Does the newspaper or journal have a good reputation?
- Do I trust the journalist?
- What will happen if I decline the invitation?

How to approach the media

This is not a book about press or public relations and so I shall only mention a few points to bear in mind if you are initiating contact with the press.

Earlier I said that the press lives on News which is a term that's hard to define. However, if your contact with the media is to succeed, your story should be original and unusual and should concern or affect sufficient people. Choosing the correct outlet for your story is important, i.e. a new development in concrete mixers won't interest the national press, but it may be a front page story for the *Builders Weekly*. Identify the news angle of your story, i.e. 500th employee has joined the company; you have received a design award for a new product; a senior executive has returned from a market expansion trip into China. Once you have a news hook, you must choose the correct outlet for it, i.e. your local newspaper or radio station may be interested in the 500th employee, particularly if you are located in an area of high unemployment; the *Design Gazette* or local TV may be interested in the design award and *Exporting Today* or the Central Office of Information may be interested in the China trip. If you are unsure which journals or newspapers are suitable for your story, consult the directories of media which are listed at the back of this book, also study the *Radio* and *TV Times* and listen to local radio stations.

Your initial approach to both print and broadcast media can be in the form of a press release, giving the gist of your story plus a contact name and number. Remember that during a telephone conversation with the broadcast media, they will be assessing *how* you're presenting yourself as well as the interest level of your story. **Enthusiasm**, **vitality** and **sincerity** are qualities which producers are always looking for.

Try to establish a continuing relationship with both your local papers and radio stations and don't be discouraged if they don't accept your first approach, which may be due to factors outside your control, i.e. lack of time or space. Local TV provides limited exposure, but it is a good learning ground, should you ever need to appear on national TV.

After you have said yes

Preparation is the key to successful interaction with the media and planning what you want to say and what you don't want to say is the first step. Remember you only have one chance to get it right and no one will be interested in your second thoughts.

In the same way as you drew an ideas map to release all your thoughts before you wrote a word of your talk, you can do the same for your media meeting. Remember to put down all the material you don't want to reveal, as well as that which you do. Code your ideas with three colours, say red for positive ideas to include, blue for points to exclude and yellow for ideas which don't fall into either category. Your red ideas will become the kernel of your interview and from them you should develop your key statements.

Target audience

In order to prepare well, you must know as much as possible about your audience. Who reads the newspaper? Who watches or listens to the programme? Talking to the *Financial Times* or the *Finchley Times* requires a different approach; talking to a reporter from the BBC Radio news desk or from *Woman's Hour* and being interviewed by a journalist from John Craven's *Newsround* (a children's news programme) or from *News at Ten* are very different situations. Find out the age, sex, education and, most important, the socio-economic group of the target audience, so you can avoid talking down to the audience or losing their interest because they don't understand you.

Now is the time to familiarize yourself with the programme. Record or video it so that you can study the style and techniques used by the presenters. Is there a bias? Is there evidence of heavy editing? Read articles in the newspaper or journal and analyse

how the interviews are handled. Is the story balanced? If possible, contact any other people who are to be interviewed on the
same subject and arrange to speak to them beforehand. If you
need more information about the programme or article, contact
the journalist involved. Find out some of the questions she
intends to ask (she won't divulge all of them), so that you can
research any additional data which you might need. Put yourself
in her place and that of the editor or producer and ask yourself
what questions they might pose. Too often my clients find it
difficult to accept that difficult questions should be anticipated
and the correct answers carefully worked out. Hoping against
hope that the journalist won't find the skeleton in your cupboard
is foolhardy. Far better to put a smart suit on your skeleton so if
the cupboards do open for a moment, it won't be recognized for
what it is. Plan how you can turn your negative points into
positive points.

Key statements

You will have decided to be interviewed because you recognized
the benefit to you or your company or both and now you must
identify how you want your audience to react. Remember the
journalist is not your audience. Your audience is made up of the
listeners, viewers or readers. Depending on the duration of
the interview, choose one or two key statements which will form
the core of your answers. Don't attempt to make more than three
points. Don't add too much – most successful replies are 20–30
seconds only. Learn to talk in brief colourful sentences. Find
illustrations and anecdotes which will capture the imagination of
your audience. Remember to avoid jargon and abbreviations
which won't be understood by the general public. When dealing
with the print media, you can afford to amplify your answers, but
bear in mind that whatever you say will be condensed, re-
arranged and even cut by sub-editors after the journalist has
written it.

Thorough preparation will enable you to put across your key
statements concisely, colourfully and entertainingly and will
reduce the possibility of misrepresentation.

Steps in your preparation:

- Research the target audience.
- Identify your key statements, i.e. what you want to say and what you don't want to say.
- Find colourful examples and anecdotes to illustrate your points.

At the radio station

The most important factor is your voice and your ability to project **enthusiasm**, **sincerity** and **vitality**.

Radio is an informal medium and you should try to concentrate on talking to the interviewer and forget the thousands or even millions who are listening to you at home. Research shows that most radio is listened to by people on their own and there is no group identity such as you'll find in a large conference hall or in a theatre. You are not addressing a group of thousands, you are talking to a number of individuals listening to you by themselves. Your words should be simple and they should paint pictures which will stir the listeners' imaginations. Try to illustrate your key statements with colourful examples.

I heard a story on the radio recently which illustrates what I mean. It was concerning the bad behaviour of drunken passengers on holiday chartered planes. A stewardess was interviewed about an occasion when a plane had to make an unscheduled landing because a passenger had become uncontrollable and was attempting to open the emergency door. In answer to a question about how the stewardess felt about these unruly passengers she said 'It is very, very upsetting for the younger girls who have never experienced such abuse. They look forward to doing this wonderful glamorous job and when they get on the plane they find it's worse than *being a barmaid in a rough pub*'. I think in a few words she painted a very clear picture.

Don't be overawed by the studio equipment or by the interviewer. You may well be in a small overheated studio with a glass wall through which the producer and technician will be sitting. Ignore the microphone and speak in a normal voice – a technician will adjust the level to your voice. Always ask to see the introduction to your appearance in order to check for inaccuracies. Also ask what the first question will be, so that you are prepared.

Speak in a steady conversational tone and avoid filler words 'You know', 'I mean' etc. and refrain from beginning every answer with 'well . . .' Don't use an impersonal style i.e. 'People think that . . .' Instead say 'I think that . . .' Being long winded and rambling is a major sin. Give brief answers which don't run over 30 seconds and pause at the end of each one to enable the interviewer to ask another question. Radio interviews are generally 2–3 minutes in length, so you only have a short time in which to deliver your message. Avoid yes/no answers and aim to put a smile in your voice. The section on questions should help you deal with the interview.

Find out before you begin, how long the interview will be so that you can pace your answers accordingly. Never speak over someone else, even to add your agreement – 'Mm that's right' – but raise your voice if someone is interrupting you and say 'May I finish . . .' If the interview is recorded and you are dissatisfied with the quality of one of your answers, ask to re-record it.

If you have a tendency to fiddle, remove any temptations such as spectacles, earrings, bracelets, paper and pens. If you need a crib, write it on a card. Nerves can make you breathless, so take a couple of deep relaxing breaths before you begin and try not to hold your breath during the interview. If the programme is recorded, make sure you know when it is scheduled for broadcast.

Television appearances

The most memorable part of your TV appearance is your own appearance. Your credibility depends almost entirely on how you look as viewers are convinced that they can instantly assess anyone within a few seconds of his appearing in their screen. In the last decade, several politicians have found to their cost that in spite of being proficient and experienced, they lost the support of the voters because their faces or personalities weren't popular on TV. It is unlikely that your career depends on a TV success but be aware that it is a very powerful medium.

Rehearse your body language

TV is very intimate. The TV camera comes closer than most of your friends. Few people look at you from a distance of only a few inches and yet a close-up on TV from your chin to your hairline reveals much of your inner feeling and thoughts. You need to build up your confidence so your uncertainty doesn't show. Remember, familiarity breeds confidence so the more you can learn about TV before your appear, the more confident you will be. Watch the programme and notice the seating arrangements and the colour of the set; study the camera angles and become aware of the cutting from one camera to another to pick up interest points; familiarize yourself with the style of interview and the types of questions which are posed.

During your practice sessions at home, try sitting in a chair similar to that which you will find in the TV studio and avoid crossing and recrossing your legs or swinging your foot. Don't fiddle with the arm of the chair – arrange your hands calmly in your lap. Put your behind well into the seat of the chair and don't slouch. While you are rehearsing in your seated position, try to put animation, enthusiasm and enjoyment into your face, but keep your head still as the camera can't keep following it if it's jerking about. If you study TV interviews and panel discussions, you'll see that most of the camera shots are head and shoulders so all your expression must be in your face.

Smile appropriately and maintain a confident and enthusiastic appearance, but be sure to match your look with the content of the interview. One politician I counselled had the unfortunate habit of smiling broadly when he discussed the problem of unemployment and was unaware of the impression he created until I recorded him on closed-circuit TV.

The point I made earlier about using your hands is doubly important on TV. Keep your hands away from your face and don't touch your hair, nose, mouth and don't fiddle with pens, jewellery or your clothing. Your hands should be still and not straightening your tie or rearranging your necklace.

Never look at the camera – in fact, try to imagine that no one else is in the studio apart from the interviewer. When you are being introduced, look at him with interest and avoid a smug or an embarrassed grin as he lists your qualities and achievements. During questions as well as when you are answering, keep your eyes on him and remember that the camera will often pick up your reaction to a question so don't grimace or pull a face. In a discussion programme, look at the speaker and try to appear interested and alert; act naturally and nod or shake your head in agreement or disagreement. Remember to keep your head up because, if the lighting is poor, you will appear to have heavy shadows under your eyes.

It may help you to control your nervousness to remember that the average audience for one TV set is three to four individuals, so imagine having a conversation with a friend in your own sitting room and try to forget the millions who may be watching you.

What to wear on TV

Try to avoid black or dark grey or even mid-blue which comes out very dark on camera as these colours can look too sombre, even for a business programme. Grey is most suitable for men but avoid white shirts and choose beige or pale blue instead. Don't wear material with any narrow stripes or checks and avoid red which can 'bleed'. Also avoid large patterns; plain colours look best on camera. Avoid jangling earrings and fussy necklines and remember that most of the camera shots will be head and shoulders so that you should aim for a simple, plain, uncluttered look. Shiny jewellery is a distraction as it catches the light. If possible, check the colour of the set before the programme so that you don't choose an outfit which clashes, or tones in so well that you disappear.

At the TV station

Adrenalin and alcohol don't mix so refuse a drink to calm your nerves as it may have the opposite effect. Take a deep breath instead or a small soft drink and remember to go to the toilet before and after your make-up session.

Make-up session

Everyone has to wear make-up on TV; without it, you will look shiny. As the lights are very hot, you will certainly perspire and give the impression you are under pressure and feeling uneasy. That's probably exactly how you will be feeling but why tell millions of people? Make-up and plenty of powder will enable you to look composed. If you are fair-haired, the lights will bleach out your colouring so expect to have your eyes made up. You should allow three-quarters of an hour for the make-up session which will be conducted by make-up experts who are also trained to calm and relax you before your appearance. If you suffer from any allergies, take your own make-up. Although you may feel very painted, particularly if you don't normally wear make-up, it won't show on camera and you will appear natural.

In the studio

When you see the studio set for the first time, you will be surprised that it looks rather tacky and smaller than it appears on your TV at home. Take a good hard look around at the lights, the cameras, the cables as well as the crew. The person in charge in the studio is the floor manager who is in contact with the director in the production control room, which is generally positioned above the studio behind a large glass wall. In the studio, there will also be an assistant floor manager, a boom operator and a minimum of three cameramen who are also in contact by headphones with the control room. In addition you'll see scene shifters and electricians. Take the opportunity of visiting the studio before your appearance if you can, to familiarize yourself with the set-up. It will seem chaotic but understanding everyone's role will help you concentrate on the interview when it's your turn so that you can avoid being distracted while on camera.

Now it's your turn

A technician will clip on a personal mike to your shirt or jacket; it's advisable for women to wear a button-through shirt or dress as high necks without a front fastening have no suitable place to which the mike can be fixed. You should also avoid wearing silk, as this can cause crackling on the mike. Table-top and boom microphones are sometimes used as backup and you can ignore them altogether.

When you are in position on the set, glance at the monitors on the floor in front of you to inspect your position on camera. Now is the time to straighten your tie, pull down your jacket and undo a button if necessary, or smoothe your skirt and check your hair. This is not vanity – you don't want your credibility to be jeopardized by a stray wisp of hair or a crooked tie. Don't perch on the edge of the chair; sit well back so that you can easily move forward or backwards. Try to maintain an open position towards the camera and when you make a gesture use the arm farthest from the camera.

Check your introduction with the interviewer if you have not done so already; inaccuracies and even the mispronunciation of your name in the first few seconds of the interview are not a good start. Also confirm the duration of the piece. If you are feeling tension around your mouth and eyes, do some exercises to release the stiffness and raise and lower your shoulders to become more relaxed. Several deep breaths will have a calming influence. Try to ignore your thumping heart and the rest of the studio, and imagine that you are about to have a private conversation with the interviewer.

The floor manager counts down from ten to zero and the interviewer faces the camera with her introduction. From now until the end of the programme, remember that the camera may be on you at any point, even when you are not talking. When the interview is over, don't thank the interviewer and *don't move*. Stay where you are until you are told you can get up. Even though sound and lights may have faded, the cameras will probably still be on the set so don't leap up and shout in relief that it's all over!

Question time

Reading a newspaper article doesn't give you much insight into the questioning techniques of the journalist, but by watching and listening to television and radio interviews you can learn more about the types of question which are often used. You will face three types of question from both print and media journalists:

1 Open questions

As part of their everyday work, managers tend to use open questions to gain as much information as possible about a situation or a subject to help them in the decision-making process, i.e. 'so what will be the outcome if we change from cardboard to plastic containers?' 'How can we cope with the new pay demands?' 'Why did you leave your last job?' Open questions are generally prefaced with What, Why, When, How, Where and Who. Both media and print journalists use them when they want ample and full answers to their questions. The purpose of the interview is to hear the interviewee's views and opinions and therefore it's the journalist's job to make sure her questions prompt interesting answers.

All the media are there to inform and to entertain and the ratio of information to entertainment varies from one programme (or paper) to another. The *News at Ten* presents a high proportion of information but with sufficient entertainment to ensure that the viewer keeps tuned to the station. On the other hand, a games show will have a higher degree of entertainment and less information. In any newsagents, you will notice the differing amounts of hard news or lightweight stories which dominate the front pages of our national dailies. The reason why I am emphasizing the element of entertainment which is present in all media is because the journalist is aware that information alone can be dull. It is in her interest, therefore, to stimulate and provoke exciting answers from you.

2 Statement questions

These questions can be answered by a yes or a no response and are generally avoided by good broadcast journalists. To illustrate this point, here is an extract from an interview with the oldest man in Birmingham recorded by a local radio journalist, in which the journalist lost control by asking the wrong kind of question.

'I expect you're very excited to be 98 years old?'

'No.'

'Well, I expect your family is very excited?'

'No.'

'I know that many people are very proud of you. Are you going to have a big party?'

'No.'

'Ninety-eight years is a grand old age and there have been many changes in Birmingham since you were born. Have you noticed a lot of changes in 98 years?'

'No.'

'You seem very healthy for your age. What's the secret of your old age?'

'Dunno!' (He might have answered – not wasting breath answering silly questions.)

As you can see, this doesn't make very exciting listening. However, statement questions in the hands of a skilled *print* journalist can become a good story.

'Were you expecting such a sharp fall in the share price?'

'No!'

'I expect it came as a bit of a shock then?'

'Yes, it did!'

'What about the future? Could the price go lower?'

'Well, yes.'

This could be written as follows: 'Gold-Top Chairman, Peter Davis, is shocked by the fall in the share price, and he predicts that there is worse to come'.

How to make your key statements

Don't try to avoid answering the question. You have probably seen and heard politicians sidestep questions and at home you find yourself saying in frustration, 'Answer the question'. Journalists are very adept at repeating and rephrasing questions and so you are ill advised to evade them. Answer the question and without pausing for breath, say 'But the point I should like to emphasize is that we have had fewer accidents in our factory than any other company in this area'. This is your key statement. You can also use phrases like 'But let me put it another way', followed by your key statement, or 'But what I think is really important is', followed by your key statement, or 'But what you shouldn't forget is', followed by your key statement.

Don't feel restricted by the questions but control the interview by adding your key statement. Remember to include anecdotes, i.e. 'I can best answer that question by telling you about an incident that happened in our Manchester Office . . .'

If you are unlucky enough to be interviewed by an inexperienced journalist, you may find that he answers his own questions. 'How do you feel about winning the contract? I expect you're very pleased. Everyone at your company must be very proud, as I know the competition was very great. It certainly is a great honour.' Try not to get drawn into this verbose nonsense and ignore his prompts. 'My company, Greystone Limited, was chosen to design and build a series of hotels in Florida and California. We think it's particularly significant that an English company and one from this area was awarded the contract, as the competition from American companies was very stiff. We feel it proves that Greystone Limited represented the best in British architecture.' Don't be self-conscious about naming your product or service, as this was one of the reasons for agreeing to a media meeting and you musn't lose sight of it. You may be looking at the interviewer but you are really talking to the audience who is listening to you at home or who will read your comments in the newspaper.

Don't wait for the right question

It may appear from this that you will never win with a journalist because he will always be in control of the questions. But remember that you are in control of the answers. You have decided what you want to say and you must say it without waiting for the right question. The right question may never come or it may come at the end of a long interview and your answer may be edited out.

In the face of hostile questioning

Everyone who is approached by the Press is concerned that they will have to defend themselves against a barrage of aggressive and abrasive questions.

Be sure you understand the difference between hard questions and hostile questions. It's the journalist's job to make an interesting programme or write an interesting article, and a cosy chat, although more comfortable for you, is dull for everyone else. The journalist represents the voice of the people so expect him to pose the questions that they would ask if put face to face with you. A reporter will often play devil's advocate to provoke a more exciting answer from you. This is an example of a bland question: 'Following your appointment as Chairman, could you describe your plans for the future of the Company?' A better, and therefore tougher, question, is 'How did you formulate the new plans for the company' or 'How do you defend your new plans for the future of the Company to those who say that they're not achievable?'

You shouldn't treat this as a confrontation and respond in an antagonistic manner. Never lose your cool. Simply stand your ground and defend your point of view in a reasonable tone with facts and not emotion. If you feel you are being asked a leading question, hold up your hand and dispute it. Don't let the interviewer get away with inaccuracies or distortions of the truth.

If the journalist discovers your weak point, you should admit it immediately. This may well disconcert him, if he was expecting you to disagree, and it will allow you sufficient time during the rest of the interview to put over some positive points, i.e. 'Yes, it is true that some of our kitchens were found to be unhygienic and had to be closed, but the point I'd like to emphasize is that we have taken the opportunity to install new equipment and have decorated throughout. Everyone will be delighted that our restaurants will be reopened in time for the Christmas parties.' Don't attempt to evade questions as journalists have a highly developed sense of smell for a good story and they will keep after you, but be prepared to turn negative points into positive statements with good explanations for apparent weaknesses.

Beware of hearing more in a question than the interviewer intends. You may well have a skeleton in the cupboard that you are worried will be dragged out for all the world to see; you may even have taken the precaution of preparing some suitable answers, but listen carefully to the question. Don't fall into the trap of answering a simple question with a detailed defensive response. Parents are often concerned with how well they will answer their children's questions about the facts of life and so the question 'Mummy, where did I come from?' is answered with a half-hour detailed biology lesson. The parent might be rather nonplussed when the child says 'Thanks, Mummy, I wanted to know 'cos Mary comes from Wales'.

Sometimes you need to reveal your hand slowly, point by point. One simple piece of information may be enough to satisfy the interviewer and if not, you still have some extra material up your sleeve. Because you have planned how you will handle problematic areas, there is no need to give the equivalent of a full scale biology lesson immediately you hear the difficult question.

Summing up with a slant

Media journalists who are anxious to leave the listener or viewer with a particular opinion will sometimes fail to summarize accurately. If you feel that you are being misrepresented, correct the interviewer immediately in a reasonable voice. Your sincerity and honesty will make a good lasting impression.

Off the record

Before the interview starts, you may tell the journalist that there is an area which you can't answer questions about. However, if during the course of the meeting he refers to it, how should you respond? Quite simply by reminding him of your agreement. 'We did agree that you wouldn't ask questions about that because of the security aspect but I am happy to talk about the rest of the project.' Interviewers will often attempt to get you to say more than you intend but remain calm and reasonable and refuse to answer, being sure to give the reason so that you don't appear to be concealing information. If you appear honest, sincere and straightforward you will gain credibility.

Don't repeat an interviewer's allegations in your denials, i.e. the interviewer might say 'It appears that the company is in difficulties and close to bankruptcy'. Your reply should contain positive statements. 'That is not so. In fact, the company is on a sound financial footing and has the full backing of the share-holders.' This is a more powerful statement than 'The company is not close to bankruptcy'.

Discussions

You'll find that the objective of a broadcast discussion is often to present a number of different points of view without necessarily reaching a specific conclusion. The choice may be left to the listener or viewer. Remember that there will be competition for air time during the discussion and you will need to feel assertive in order to make your points.

Before you agree to take part, find out who else is on the programme and what viewpoints they represent. The producers may seek to present a stimulating programme by having a contrast of opinions and so you shouldn't expect to find fellow souls on the panel.

In order to present your opinions forcefully, you must have sufficient data to support them and to counteract arguments from your opponents. Also remember to research into their back-grounds for further ammunition.

Discussions are often pre-recorded so that the dull patches can be edited, resulting in a more enjoyable and entertaining pro-gramme. Make sure you speak in headlines and don't ramble. Listen attentively to distinguish between evidence, argument and conclusions; examine the evidence offered by the other speakers to see if it is relevant or consistent; look at the assumptions underlying their conclusions to see if they are logical and lastly, add a touch of humour to persuade your audience.

Telephone interviews

Print interviews are often conducted over the phone. However, if the journalist is unknown to you, try to persuade him to talk to you face to face. In this way, you are in more control of the situation and can judge how much it is advisable to say. Radio interviews are sometimes conducted over the phone when the story is hot news, but before you begin you should establish the parameters of the interview as well as the time limit. Talk in short punchy sentences and in a normal tone of voice.

Unless you find yourself at the centre of a major news story in an inaccessible part of the world, you are unlikely to be interviewed over the phone for TV. However, interviews are occasionally conducted in a regional studio by a national interviewer in, say, London. Respond to the interviewer as if he were in the room with you and try to look animated and lively as the camera records your responses.

Interviews in the office

If you are fortunate enough to be offered an interview in your office, accept it. You will feel more confident when you are on home ground and it is less time consuming. Radio interviews are often conducted in offices or hotel rooms with little disruption to the normal routine, except to ban telephone calls and to switch off background noise such as air conditioning or heating. TV recordings are more disruptive, as additional people and equipment are involved and they may need to move your furniture in order to provide a suitable background. Make sure that constant cups of tea and coffee are available and you will be popular with everyone.

Press conferences

These are called to respond to bad news or to announce good news.

If a negative story breaks about your company or organization, you may want to call a press conference to refute the story or to present your own angle. Think carefully of the benefit of this because you may be in danger of prolonging a small one-day story into a larger two- or three-day exposure. If a press conference seems the correct path, open with a brief statement that conveys your company's objective. This press statement should also be in a written form, so that it can be handed out to journalists. You may choose to have two or three spokesmen present to answer questions but ensure that a time limit is imposed from the beginning.

Good news is more fun for you but less newsworthy and so, to attract a good attendance, you must make it a special occasion. There is considerable competition for journalists' time so plan an original incentive to draw them. The services of a good public relations company are always beneficial in all your interactions with the press and if you find you are appearing more frequently, consider a short course in media training which will build your confidence and add a polish to your performance.

A last word

Remember to treat all journalists with respect but not reverence or familiarity. You are the expert so listen to the question, answer it concisely and include your key statements, but challenge any misleading information.

Summary: how to meet the media

- Discover the reason for the invitation.
- What's in it for you?
- Prepare thoroughly.
- Watch or listen to the programme. Read the newspaper.
- Rehearse, rehearse and rehearse.
- Remain cool, calm and confident – you are the expert.

20 Final thoughts

As I write the last few pages of this book it reminds me of how you might feel the day after a particularly important speech. For weeks, maybe even months, it has been on your mind. Sometimes in the forefront as you grappled with the right choice of words; sometimes in the background as you watched a television programme and realized that you could use an amusing line from a comedy show. Then suddenly it's over. It took months to prepare and only moments to deliver. It might seem like a runner who prepares for a hundred yard sprint at the Olympic Games. In fact speaking is not like that at all. There is no winner in the speaking game. You may win or lose a contract, but not entirely on your presentation skills. Rarely is speaking a one-off event. Developing your ability to speak effectively is a continuous process.

Now you've read this book, you will see its basic difficulty: that you can't learn to speak just by reading. Trying to do so would be like trying to learn to ride a bike from a book. I've written about the techniques but that is only a tiny fraction of effective speaking. Now you are able to identify all the parts of the bike, you understand the principles of balance and where you should put your hands and your feet. You know how to indicate where you're going. Now is the moment to hop on and have a ride.

Reading this book or any other won't make you a good speaker, but practising will. Unfortunately, unlike bike riding, you can't use a quiet back street to learn the basics of speaking. You need an audience to judge its effectiveness. They will be there to see all your attempts to keep your balance and to witness the occasional crash. But crashes are part of the learning process. If you've ever watched a baby learning to walk you'll know that initial failures are inevitable. The trick is not to be discouraged. Imagine a baby saying to itself as it fell back on its bottom for the umpteenth time

'I'll never get the hang of this. I'm just making a fool of myself, I'll have to give up'. You must keep at it.

If you feel shy, search out non-work-related occasions to speak, i.e. to the sixth form at your old school, at the local sports club, or to the residents' association. If you are totally inexperienced set yourself the goal of asking a question at your next meeting. I have known speakers who attend public meetings with the sole objective of asking a question. They sit close to the front so that they can't be ignored. As soon as question time is announced, up shoot their hands to 'speak in public'. If you decide to practise like this you will probably find you experience the same symptoms of nervousness as you do when you are giving a talk. Your heart will beat faster and you'll have a dry mouth and sweaty palms. Acknowledge all your feelings, don't try to fight them. Be aware of your physical state, but don't allow it to control you. In a meeting at work when you have no specific role, ensure that you speak up within the first ten minutes. The longer you leave it the more difficult it will be to contribute. Simply offer agreement, i.e. 'Yes that's true, we've noticed that too' or ask for more information, i.e. 'Could you give me an example of how that happened'. Speaking up early will establish your presence and make it easier for you to speak again.

As you become more proficient, consider volunteering to chair a meeting or to give a vote of thanks at your social club. Each occasion will be a challenge and an opportunity to become familiar with your anxiety. Turn it into positive energy to stimulate original thoughts and entertaining ideas.

If you are an experienced speaker you probably know already how you could become more effective. Maybe there is only one reason why this doesn't happen. Lack of time. You know that you should pay more attention to your preparation. You realize you should rehearse. You understand the value of good visual aids but you don't have the time. No one can change that but you. The presentations and talks that you give may not be crucial to you and your company but if you want to improve as a speaker you'll need to make the time for it. Going on courses or reading books won't change you from being a mediocre speaker into an exceptional one. Only you can do that.

Effective speakers find time to prepare and practise, but the most vital part of a good speaker is much more difficult to acquire. It's in their hearts and shines out for everyone to appreciate. It's the magical quality of enjoyment. In other chapters I have stressed **enthusiasm**, **sincerity** and **vitality**. These are all based on the speaker's ability to enjoy communicating with his or her audience. Enjoyment is contagious. The audience will enjoy your talk if you enjoy giving it.

Thank you for being a good listener. I suspect you haven't agreed with everything I've said but I hope that some of my suggestions will help you to capture the butterflies and train them to fly in formation.

This is a personal selection of books and companies which I have found helpful. It is not intended as a complete list. Although many of the companies are London based, they operate throughout Great Britain.

Further reading

How to Set Up and Run Conferences and Meetings
Daily Telegraph, London

Improving Presentation Skills Michael Stevens
Kogan Page, London

Our Master's Voice Max Atkinson
Methuen & Co. Ltd, London

Promoting Yourself on Television and Radio Michael Bland and Simone Mondesir
Kogan Page, London

Public Speakers Treasure Chest H & H Prochnow
Thorsons Publishers Ltd, Wellingborough, Northants

Teach Yourself Body Language Gordon R Wainwright
Hodder & Stoughton, London

The Book of Wit and Humour Peter Cagney
Thorsons Publishers Ltd, Wellingborough, Northants.

The Business Guide to Effective Speaking Jacqueline Dunckel and Elizabeth Parnham
Kogan Page, London

Your Voice and How to Use It Successfully Cicely Berry
Harrap, London

Useful addresses

Press directories

Benn's Media Directory
Benn's Business Information Service Ltd
PO Box 20
Sovereign Way
Tonbridge
Kent
TN9 12Q

Willings Press Guide
Thompson Skinner Directories
Windsor Court
East Grinstead House
East Grinstead
West Sussex
RH19 1XE

Training in presentation skills

British Institute of Management
Management House
Cottingham Road
Corby
Northants NN17 1TT

0536 204222

Communication Results
Station House
Station Road
Bourton on the Water
Glos GL54 2ER

0451 20160

Cranfield School of Management
Cranfield
Bedford MK43 0AL

0234 751122

CTVC
Hillside Studios
Merry Hill Road
Bushey
Herts WD2 1DR

01-950 4426

Industrial Society
Peter Range House
3 Carlton House Terrace
London SW1Y 5DG

01-839 4300

Monadnock International Ltd
2 The Chapel
Royal Victoria Patriotic Building
Fitzhugh Grove
London SW18 3SX

01-871 2546

Speakeasy Training Ltd
17 Clifton Road
London N3 2AS

01-346 2776

Wadlow Grosvenor Presentation Training
19/20 Grosvenor Street
London W1X 9FD

01-409 1225

Training films on presentation skills

Melrose Film Production Ltd
8–12 Queen St
London SW1H 9HP

01-222 1744

Rank Ltd
PO Box 70 Great West Road
Brentford
Middx TW8 9HR

01-568 9222

Video Arts
Dumbarton House
68 Oxford Street
London W1N 9LA

01-637 7288

Visual aids materials

Bell & Howell Ltd
Alperton House
Bridgewater Road
Wembley
Middlesex HA0 1EG

01-902 8812

Kroy/Business Machines Ltd
Royston House
267 Cranmore Boulevard
Shirley
Solihull
W Midlands B90 4QT

021 745 5529

Letraset UK Ltd
195–203 Waterloo Road
London SE1

01-928 7551

3M United Kingdom plc
3M House
PO Box 1
Bracknell
Berks RG12 1JU

National Audio Visual Aids Library
Paxton Place
Gipsy Road
London SE27 9SR

01-670 4247

Sasco
27 Hastings Road
Bromley
Kent BR2 8NA

01-462 2241

Equipment to hire

Autocue Conferences Ltd
Autocue House
265 Merton Road
London SW18 5JS

01-870 0104

Audio Visual Equipment Ltd
16 Southsea Rd
Kingston-upon-Thames
Surrey

01-549 7521

Eurocom
Elcom House
20 Westminster Square
Durham Street
London SE11 5JA
01-582 2669

Visual aid producers

Art UnLtd
3 Bedford Street
London WC2E 9HD

01-379 0323

Enlightment AV & Video Productions
Warren's Lane
Botesdale
Diss
Norfolk IP22 1BW

Nobo Visual Aids Ltd
Alder Close
Eastbourne
East Sussex BN23 6GB

0323 641521

Slideformat
273 Regent Street
London W1

01-491 2515

Visual Aids Centre Ltd
7 Garrick Street
London WC2E 9AR

01-240 8875

Useful books of instant artwork

Business & Industry Ad Lib
Cartoons Ad Lib
Borders Ad Lib
Artwork Ad Lib

The Hinwood Libraries of Ideas
Crossways Road
Graysholt
Hindhead
Surrey GU29 6HE

0428 73 4573

Speaking clubs

Association of Speakers Clubs
for further information phone:
0943 464589

International Training in Communication
(ITC)
Joe Mankowitz
26 Longridge Road
London sw5 9sj

01-373 0788

Toastmasters International
Suite 4
37 Christchurch Ave
London nw6 7bd

01-451 2292

Script writer

Jon Rollason
43 Queenswood Court
Kings Ave
London sw4 8eb

01-674 8959

Personality speakers

Associated Speakers
24A Park Road
Hayes
Middlesex
ub4 8jn

01-848 9048

Ivor Spencer
12 Little Bournes
Alleyn Park
Dulwich
London se21

01-670 8424

Prime Performers
The Studio
5 Kidderpore Avenue
London NW3 73X

01-431 0211

Conference venues

Conference Care
1 Union Street
Bedford

0234 327766

The Conference Office
Imperial College
Exhibition Road
London SW7 2AZ

Index

Index

Kathryn Redway
Rapid Reading £4.99

Why buy and read this book?

Many of us have large amounts of literature to deal with – papers, books, documents, reports. But how much of our time do we actually need to spend reading them?

In this concise and effective guide Kathryn Redway – for the last five years a leading management consultant – gives you the techniques to revolutionise your reading.

She shows how to speed up your reading rate – while at the same time increasing understanding and effectively assimilating the information relevant to you.

Rapid Reading leaves old attitudes and unrewarding reading habits behind. Here are the techniques and exercises that will improve concentration, maximise existing skills and intensify memory.

All these books are available at your local bookshop or newsagent, or can be ordered direct from the publisher. Indicate the number of copies required and fill in the form below.

Send to: **CS Department, Pan Books Ltd., P.O. Box 40, Basingstoke, Hants.   RG21 2YT.**

or phone: 0256 469551 (Ansaphone), quoting title, author and Credit Card number.

Please enclose a remittance* to the value of the cover price plus: 60p for the first book plus 30p per copy for each additional book ordered to a maximum charge of £2.40 to cover postage and packing.

*Payment may be made in sterling by UK personal cheque, postal order, sterling draft or international money order, made payable to Pan Books Ltd.

Alternatively by Barclaycard/Access:

Card No.

Signature:

Applicable only in the UK and Republic of Ireland.

While every effort is made to keep prices low, it is sometimes necessary to increase prices at short notice. Pan Books reserve the right to show on covers and charge new retail prices which may differ from those advertised in the text or elsewhere.

NAME AND ADDRESS IN BLOCK LETTERS PLEASE:

....

Name————————————————————————————

Address————————————————————————————

————————————————————————————————

————————————————————————————————

————————————————————————————————

3/87